Hitler's Attack U-Boats

Hitler's Attack U-Boats

THE KRIEGSMARINE'S SUBMARINE STRIKE FORCE

JAK P MALLMANN SHOWELL

FRONTLINE
BOOKS

HITLER'S ATTACK U-BOATS
The Kriegsmarine's Submarine Strike Force

First published in Great Britain in 2020 by

Frontline Books
An imprint of
Pen & Sword Books Ltd
Yorkshire - Philadelphia

Copyright © Jak P Mallmann Showell, 2020

ISBN 978 1 52677 101 8

The right of Jak P Mallmann Showell to be identified as the author of this work has been asserted by him in accordance with the Copyright, Designs and Patents Act 1988.

A CIP catalogue record for this book is available from the British Library

All rights reserved. No part of this book may be reproduced or transmitted in any form or by any means, electronic or mechanical including photocopying, recording or by any information storage and retrieval system, without permission from the Publisher in writing.

Typeset in 10.5/13 pt Palatino
by Aura Technology and Software Services, India.

Printed and bound in the UK by TJ International Ltd.

Pen & Sword Books Ltd incorporates the Imprints of Aviation, Atlas, Family History, Fiction, Maritime, Military, Discovery, Politics, History, Archaeology, Select, Wharncliffe Local History, Wharncliffe True Crime, Military Classics, Wharncliffe Transport, Leo Cooper, The Praetorian Press, Remember When, Seaforth Publishing and Frontline Publishing.

For a complete list of Pen & Sword titles please contact

PEN & SWORD BOOKS LTD
47 Church Street, Barnsley, South Yorkshire, S70 2AS, England
E-mail: enquiries@pen-and-sword.co.uk
Website: www.pen-and-sword.co.uk

Or

PEN AND SWORD BOOKS
1950 Lawrence Rd, Havertown, PA 19083, USA
E-mail: Uspen-and-sword@casematepublishers.com
Website: www.penandswordbooks.com

Contents

Introduction······vi

Chapter 1	Attack U-boats of the Second World War	1
Chapter 2	Lessons Learned from the First World War	3
Chapter 3	The Aftermath of the First World War	12
Chapter 4	Early Developments	19
Chapter 5	The Second World War in a Nutshell	38
Chapter 6	1935: The New Generation of Attack U-boats	43
Chapter 7	Attack U-boats: Their Main External Features	57
Chapter 8	Internal Features of a Type VIIC	116
Chapter 9	The Crew: Key U-boat Positions	121
Chapter 10	Operational Command	224
Appendix 1	Wartime Statistics	230
Appendix 2	The Attack U-boat Fleet	234
Appendix 3	Technical Data	238
Appendix 4	German Wartime Ranks	244

Glossary 246
Index 261

Introduction

This book has been produced to help study the Battle of the Atlantic; therefore it does not include the great detail required by model makers. Hopefully it has found the right balance between presenting enough technical information to understand what was happening at sea without going into too many specialised subjects. Naval vocabulary can be rather daunting, especially when it is in a foreign language, and complicated compound nouns that appear as one word in German have been split up with flowing hyphens or tildes (~) to make reading easier. I hope this will not upset readers who are fluent in German.

Most of the material for this book has come from the German U-boat Museum in Cuxhaven-Altenbruch and I should like to thank its founder and director, Horst Bredow, for his help. I am also grateful to a multitude of other museums that have provided information and are well worth a visit. Information about their locations, opening times and contact details can be found on the Internet.

The museums mentioned in this book, all worth more than just one visit, are:

Deutsches U-Boot-Museum, Cuxhaven-Altenbruch.
International Maritime Museum of Hamburg.
Maschinen Museum, Kiel-Wik.
Marine Ehrenmal, Laboe near Kiel with *U-995* as museum.
U-Boot Ehrenmal, Möltenort near Kiel.
Deutsches Marinemuseum, Wilhelmshaven.
Vesikko Museum, Suomenlinna (Helsinki), Finland.
Museum of Science and Industry, Chicago, USA.
D-2 Museum, St. Petersburg, Russia.
Aeronauticum Museum, Cuxhaven–Nordholz.

INTRODUCTION

U-534 Museum, Woodside Ferry Terminal, Birkenhead. (Merseyside Maritime Museum, Liverpool with Battle of the Atlantic display, and Western Approaches Headquarters, Liverpool, are both nearby.)

Bletchley Park, Milton Keynes – a short distance north of London.

Zeebrugge Maritime Museum, Belgium.

Chapter 1

Attack U-boats of the Second World War

Germany had three main types of attack U-boats during the Second World War:

- Type II: Small coastal boats.
- Type VII: Medium-sized seagoing boats.
- Type IX: Large ocean-going double-hulled boats.

When an initial design was improved, a letter was added after the Roman numeral to identify each new version. There was also a Type I, similar to the Type VII, but only two of them were built and none survived the war.

All three have roots going back to the First World War as follows:

- Type II was based on the Type UB II of 1915 and Type UF of 1918 and had a forerunner *Vesikko* that was built in Finland.
- Type VII was based on the Type UB III of 1915–16 and had a forerunner *Vetehinen* that was also built in Finland.
- Type IX was developed from *U-81* of 1915 and an early version, the Russian *D-2*, was built in Leningrad (now St. Petersburg again) from German plans.

Pre-First World War U-boats were identified with the letter 'U' for *Unter~see~boot* (undersea boat) followed by a number, but there was also an export version on the stocks, which was labelled UB to distinguish it from the others. The letters UB followed by an operational number were later also used to identify the first *wartime* emergency attack submarines, built initially for hitting at Britain's cross-Channel supply routes. Later, when special minelaying U-boats were ordered, they received the identification of UC. A plain 'U' remained in use for boats that had roots going back to the pre-war development process.

Chapter 2

Lessons Learned from the First World War

At the beginning of the First World War it became obvious that high quality, sophisticated production was going to give way to designs that could be built quickly and then be manned by inexperienced men with the minimum of training. The first wartime UB and UC concepts had hardly been put on the drawing boards when fresh demands snowballed

UB-122, launched on 2 February 1918 in Bremen, under tow. Take away the serrated net cutter on the bows, the two masts supporting the radio aerial and the 88mm gun and one could have difficulties distinguishing this 1917 boat with the Type VII of the Second World War.

in from the front. As a result hundreds of different specifications were considered and the initial UB project gave way to UB II and even a much larger UB III. These slightly bigger UB III boats are of special interest because they were developed to hit British shipping far out in the Western Approaches, with the capability to go on further into the deepest Atlantic. Astonishingly enough, the primitive boats that appeared there were incredibly successful. They terrified the whole world by threatening to cut off and starve the biggest maritime power into submission and despite many drawbacks, they got pretty close to this objective.

The UB III project

It might be of interest to compare these early boats with the later Type VII, which was developed from them. Miraculously one example of this early UB III attack submarine survives and is still lying in the mud of the Medway Estuary, a short distance east of London.

UB-48–UB-53 were the first of this new design, which continued to run through several stages of development before the later version, made up of *UB-118* to *UB-132*, was launched a few months before the end of the First World War. Although appearing at the very end of the war, some of them did see operational service under the harshest of conditions.

UB-40 being scrapped in Ostend (Belgium) after the First World War.

	UB III UB-48–UB-53	**UB III** UB-118–UB-132	**VIIB** U-45
First launched:	6 Jan 1917	13 Dec 1917	27 Apr 1938
Displacement:	516/651t	512/643t	753/1,040t
Length:	55.3m	55.9m	66.5m
Beam:	5.8m	5.8m	6.2m
Depth:	3.7m	3.7m	4.7m
Diving depth:	50m	50m	100–200m
Speed surface:	13.5kt	13.9kt	17.9kt
Speed dived:	8kt	7.6kt	8kt
Range surface:	9,050nm @ 6kt	7,280nm @ 6kt	8,700nm @ 10kt
Range dived:	55nm @ 4kt	55nm @ 4kt	90nm @ 4kt
Torpedo tubes:	4 bow	4 bow	4 bow
	1 stern	1 stern	1 stern
Guns:	1 × 88mm	1 × 88mm	1 × 88mm
	1 × 105mm		1 × 20mm AA
Crew:	34	34	44

UB-49, launched on 6 January 1917. The flag with what could be red, white and blue stripes could be that of Schleswig-Holstein, Germany's most northerly province where Kiel is located. This is identical to the flag of The Netherlands.

UB-57 being launched in Bremen on 21 June 1917.

The left-hand column of the table on page 5 gives details of the first UB III boats that were launched, the centre column of the later version of the same type but with modifications, and the right-hand column of the first Type VIIB. The reason for comparing the two First World War boats with a Type VIIB is that the Type VIIA did not have an internal stern torpedo tube and the Type VIIB was laid down before the first Type VIIA was launched. So the Type VIIA and VIIB designs were conceived at about the same time. Later Type VIIB boats were provided with a slightly improved performance to become the Type VIIC.

Shortly after the end of the First World War, a large number of surrendered U-boats were brought to Britain where some of them were taken from one coastal port to another for a general inspection by anyone interested in seeing their interiors. Following this they were passed on to scrap merchants to exploit. These war-torn boats were quite valuable because they contained expensive copper wiring and many of their fittings were made from brass or phosphor bronze. So, with least six boats in the Medway Estuary, there were ample profitable opportunities for recycling.

The surrendered U-boats made a direct contribution to the gloomy post-war economy, with many items being sold off as military surplus. A cement

UB-126 after the surrender. One wonders how the helmsman could have steered the boat from such an absurd position and why the wheel was not placed behind the shelter of the conning tower wall. The gun had a calibre of 88mm.

works at Halling (on the River Medway south of Rochester), which acquired the diesel engines from *UB-122*, had them delivered by taking the whole submarine up river at high tide so that the dismantling could take place close to where the heavy engines were required. While doing this, it was also necessary to remove the batteries in the bows to balance the boat and to allow it to float back to the estuary. By removing this heavy ballast, the entire hulk became too unstable and, to make boat handling even more difficult, a huge hole had been cut in the engine room for lifting out the machinery. It would seem that a pontoon was attached to each side to prevent the now-precarious hull from rolling over and filling with water.

The last step in the recycling process was to move the unwanted remains of the steel hulk to an out-of-the-way wreck depository where they could be sunk in deep water. It would appear that some enterprising rag-and-bone man or scrap merchant came up with a rather fascinating idea for making a little extra money at this stage of the proceedings. There was so much iron and steel around at the end of the war that no one was terribly interested in recycling it. Yet, it would seem likely that the attractive non-ferrous torpedo tubes were still inside the hull because their external doors were part of the tubes rather than the boat's structure and removing them would result in massive 53cm-diameter holes being left below the waterline.

Looking at the position of the wreck, it is highly likely that it was beached deliberately on what is one of the few isolated pieces of high ground in the estuary. The front of the bows are lying close to the wreck, suggesting that this part was cut off while lying on this little island. By having beached the hulk at high tide, it was possible to return at low tide to remove the valuable brass torpedo tubes, which would have fetched a considerable sum from any scrap metal merchant.

The wreck of *UB-122* on a high point in the Medway estuary, just north of East Hoo Creek. This is less than half a kilometre north of what was the longest British pier called Bee Ness Jetty, which carried a pipeline from Kingsnorth power station to the deep-water channel so that tankers could deliver oil and bitumen for the power station's boilers.

Close-up of *UB-122*'s hull as it was in 2014 when visited by a BBC camera team.

The pressure hull with the remains of the double hull that was originally wrapped around it. The tanks of the double hull were open to seawater so that the pressure inside them would always be the same as the water pressure on the outside and could therefore be made from thin steel. The pressure hull was made from high-quality steel that was considerably thicker.

The hole into which the torpedo tube used to fit. These tubes were made from expensive brass or phosphor bronze and were therefore removed by scrap merchants after the war.

The front of *UB-122* lying in the mud of the Medway with the holes for the two upper torpedo tubes just visible.

Following extensive research it would seem that the wreck in the Medway Estuary is *UB-122* and that this is the only almost complete U-boat from the First World War to be visible for much of the time. Only very high tides hide it from view for short periods. This is by no means the only U-boat wreck, but it is the most accessible and all the others have had the tops of their steel hull removed, leaving only the ribs of the lower section stuck in the ground.

The mud at *UB-122*'s resting site is much more than treacherous. It is a killer capable of swallowing even good swimmers who venture into it. The local fire brigade carries special inflatable matting for when they have rescue people from the mud's clutches and locals treat the creeks with the greatest of respect. They are death traps for anyone not acquainted with the muddy conditions. The wreck lies more than a kilometre from the nearest firm ground and the mud there is soft enough to drown anyone attempting to walk out to it.

It looks as if the scrap merchants missed some of the non-ferrous metal or these bits were just too heavy to carry away in a small boat. Various bits and pieces can still be seen to be lurking among the mud and one wonders what else might be hidden below the soft silt that now covers much of the site.

Chapter 3

The Aftermath of the First World War

Despite considerable interest in submarines, records of what went on during the years following the First World War appear to have been stored in a bucket of sludge and have now sunk into the murk of time. Most of them have probably been destroyed. What we are left with are piles of one-sided and somewhat misleading propaganda, generated by those who won the majority of battles and we do not know precisely what people were doing in their private backyards. We do know that much of Western Europe was fixated on the powerful theme of the Great War having been 'the war to end all wars' and there would be no more in the future. By the end of the 1920s, this was so deeply ingrained that the Imperial War Museum in London was instructed not to collect any current material but to concentrate on presenting the history of the Great War. No doubt such views, together with a deep worldwide recession, also contributed to a lethargic attitude as far as new submarine construction was concerned.

Britain and the other victors may have been aloof from what was going on in Europe, but things appeared slightly different when looking at them from different perspectives. The Russians were peeved because their successful revolution had also cut them off from the rest of the world and the countries still being led by royalty kept a cool distance. Russia had also seen how the Western Powers managed to encroach into Europe and the leaders of the shaky revolution feared that this power might be turned against them in the future. So, suitable precautions had to be taken. Other, smaller countries weren't terribly happy either. Peace may have broken out in Europe, but there was still enough tension to worry about. The new nations created by the

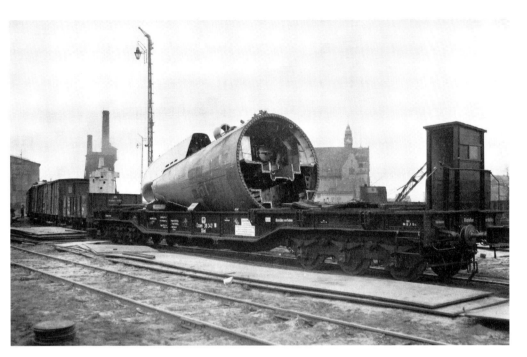

The bow section and part of the conning tower of *UB-10* prior to being moved from Bremen to an assembly yard in Antwerp (Belgium) for operations against British cross-Channel transports. This was a single-hull type where the pressure hull formed the outside skin of the boat. One of the two bow torpedo tubes is just visible. The deck on which the crew walked is about halfway up the circular section and the empty space below it shows the inside of what probably is a compensating or torpedo tank. Note the conning tower section in the next wagon. The hut at the end of the special railway carriage was a shelter for a brakeman who was there to assist with slowing down the heavy weight. Loading these trains required very precise positioning before passing through a tunnel gauge with the narrowest dimensions that were likely to be encountered en-route. *UB-10* was one of the forerunners of the Finnish *Vesikko*, which was further developed to become the Type II of the Second World War.

Allies by hiving off land from Russia, Austria-Hungary and Germany, showed signs of great instability, with the new governments often being incapable of providing even basic necessities for civilized life. Electricity, gas, transport, food, clothing, heating, protection from criminals and so forth were often in incredibly short supply. To cap it all, there was considerable ethnic conflict with enough persecution of the underdog in those new countries to worry their older, more established

The first U-boats were launched before there were radios for them, but this new communications equipment had taken its place as an essential part of their armoury by the time the First World War started. The big problem was that it was still quite unreliable, with no guarantees that messages would reach their destination. In this photograph the two high masts, looking like elongated, old-fashioned tennis racquets, supported the aerial wires and had to be lowered before the boat could dive.

neighbours. Despite many complaints, often several per week flooding into the headquarters of the Red Cross in Switzerland, the victorious Allies cowered in the shadows and did very little or nothing to stem the increase of ethnic violence throughout the new states which they had created. This made many a small nation deeply frightened of what was going on around them.

Finland, for example, wasn't sure who her allies were or whether she had any significant ones she could count on. Following her independence from Russia in 1918, the country remained surrounded by turbulence and saw no reasons for sitting quietly on any laurels dished out at the end of the Great War. To make matters worse, people in Finland were horrified when, immediately after having been founded as an independent nation, the Polish army invaded Russia, apparently in the hope of expanding its frontiers further eastwards. If such a small country had the audacity to tackle a so much bigger neighbour, then smaller nations saw themselves seriously threatened. Spain was also not terribly happy and hoping that something might happen which would bring the Rock of Gibraltar back under her sovereignty. In addition to this, a civil war was brewing within that country and one didn't have to travel much further along the Mediterranean to find more hotbeds of discontent. The British Gurkha Board of Honours for the First World War, for example, shows soldiers being killed in action as late as 1921, which helps to explain why the squabbles between Greece and Turkey and the troubles in Palestine made many people feel uneasy. There was enough commotion in all corners of the world for many nations to be eagerly seeking ways of protecting themselves from voracious neighbours.

Those nations which were considering building new submarines didn't have to wait long for the final results of the First World War to be published. Britain, the United States and Germany produced lengthy accounts and U-boats had been such a major issue that their performance was analysed in the greatest detail. What was more, ordinary people had been instilled with such irrational fear of the dreaded U-boats that the media started bombarding the general public with the news that the new anti-submarine weapons were making such good progress that they would render future submarine operations impossible. The media told the world that the disasters of the Great War could never be repeated. Never again would Britain have its supply routes cut off. The Allied Submarine Detection Investigation Committee had produced a device (Asdic), which would find submerged submarines as easily as lookouts spotting ships on the surface. Submarines could no longer hide below the waves and new anti-submarine weapons were going to blast them out of the water. So the general public was given the impression that the dreaded submarine had come to the end of its effective life.

Despite such rhetoric, it is most interesting to note that there had hardly been an effective way of dealing with U-boats and no real weapon capable of sinking them had been invented. Depth charges had made an appearance towards the end of the war, but accounted for only about 24 boats sunk out of a total of about 150. As one naval officer put it, 'What's the point of dropping bombs on submarines, if you don't know where they are?' Mines had been responsible for dealing with the highest proportion, sinking some forty-five U-boats. The next highest number was the most worrying; thirty-five U-boats had disappeared without trace and without the cause being known. It seemed highly likely that malfunctioning machinery and human error were to blame.

The years following the First World War saw considerable research. On the one hand new anti-submarine weapons were eagerly devised and on the other engineers were producing better machinery, to make individual parts within submarines more reliable. In addition to this they incorporated fail-safe systems for when men didn't follow the correct procedures. Not all of these came about as a result of war experiences. The Thetis Catch, a device that prevented torpedo tubes from bursting open if they were accidentally unlocked while full of water, was just one example.

This post-war submarine development was taking place at a time when the industrial nations of the entire world were in poor shape. The Allies may have won the First World War; but that conflict had changed the way individuals lived. People were no longer willing to work for long hours for little money in subservient positions. Even the soldiers from the victorious nations came home to find themselves sliding down a slippery path into recession. The peace after the Great War was of an oppressive nature. Economic depression and unrest dictated that the ordinary people in both Britain and the United States were going to be living on the breadline and a good proportion of workers were dependent on handouts from the state and from charities. Things were even worse in Germany and in Russia, where hunger, poverty and then rampant inflation hit the working classes especially hard. Perhaps it is no wonder that the leading naval powers did not devote a great deal of time and energy to developing new submarines.

The peace treaty of the First World War prohibited Germany from owning submarines or building them for export. This was a damaging blow for her industries, which were among the leaders in this field.

THE AFTERMATH OF THE FIRST WORLD WAR

UB-65 of the First World War, one of the forerunners of the Type VII U-boats. It is surprising how modern some of the old boats looked. Many of the Second World War features were already there and there were no great differences in performance between the two generations. Perhaps the biggest modification, as far as the men were concerned, was that power-assisted machinery had become standard in the bigger boats by 1939, so that there was no longer any need to rely on human muscle power alone to turn the many wheels that needed constant adjustment.

The German Navy certainly had more experience with submarines than any other nation. Perhaps it is no wonder that Finland, Spain and Turkey were keen to look to this German expertise to build its future submarines. German specialists set up shop in Holland as a commercial shipbuilding venture and from there explored the possibilities of building boats in foreign countries. These days it is difficult to judge how much of this was known by the Western Allies, but enough rumblings remain in print to suggest that there were strong fears of secret German developments taking place in Russia. Russia, suffering from extreme problems of hunger and deprivation as a result of both the war and its own revolution, had surrendered to Germany on 3 March 1918 with the Treaty of Brest-Litovsk. So, the guns of the Eastern Front fell silent more than six months before the West and before the humiliation of the Treaty of Versailles. Details of this treaty had only just been made public when British naval experts voiced deep concerns that Germany was in a good position to continue building submarines in Russian shipyards, despite them having been on opposite sides during the war. Unfortunately the secrecy which cloaked activities in Russia remained in place for more than half a century and many of the British and American assessments were written during the Cold War, when it was extremely difficult to obtain information from the Soviet Union.

As far as technology was concerned, the First World War not only changed the way people thought and lived but it also refined precision engineering to set off a mechanical revolution. Machines were replacing horses and industry was being dominated by human brainpower rather than by sweat and muscles. This gave rise to an era of incredible inventions, which snowballed so rapidly that one new concept often triggered off many new opportunities in other fields. Unfortunately the economic recession resulted in not much being done with many of the new inventions. This is certainly true as far as submarine development was concerned. The upshot of this was that engineers refined the individual features to make submarines work better, but most projects didn't get much further than the drawing board.

Chapter 4

Early Developments

Whilst paintings have been traded for high prices for a long time, the value of technology has hardly been recognised and as a result many of the early inventions that changed the world have been disposed of when they came to the end of their effective lives, to be lost forever. *Vesikko* and *D-2* are important survivors from the chain of technological progress because they slot into a transitional stage of submarine development. Their engines and motors and many of the other features were reasonably well advanced, but their control systems had not yet caught up with what became standard for the Second World War. That meant brains and human efficiency combined with muscle power were still essential for making the machinery function because the more modern fail-safe and power-assisted systems had not yet been invented.

a. The Finnish *Vesikko*

The gulf separating Finland from Estonia is only about 100km (60 miles) wide and the ice in it can be thick enough to support cars and lorries for several months in winter. On top of this, the coast is guarded by what looks like a mass of sandbanks. Some of these are not high enough to break through the surface of the water while others support a multitude of trees. The problem with them is that they are not composed of sand but of hard, granite-like rock, which means that bumping into them can be more than merely inconvenient. These two natural barriers make it obvious that the coast is no playground for large, unmanoeuvrable ships, especially when they are being chased by small, agile torpedo boats. So, it is perhaps no wonder that the fledgling Finnish navy looked at two types of submarine: one big enough to operate in open waters further away from home and another, smaller boat capable

of dodging around the natural hazards of coastal waters. The navy turned to Germany to develop both of these. The larger type was easier to build and three boats, *Vetehinen*, *Vesihiisi* and *Iku-Turso*, were laid down as early as 1926 with help of the German development bureau then based in Holland because Germany was still not allowed any form of submarine development. These designs were later further developed in Germany to become the famous Type VII, the largest class of submarine ever built.

Left and below: The Finnish *Vesikko*, now a museum in Suomenlinna (Helsinki), was originally known by its construction number of CV707.

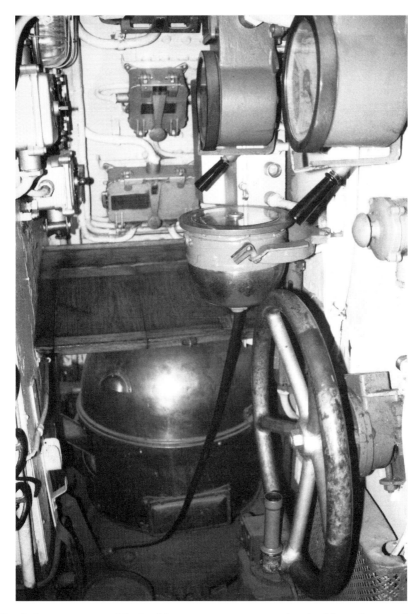

The helmsman steered by looking at a gyrocompass that had been invented by the French only a few years earlier. This system was controlled by machinery inside the large tub-like container on the floor and has a cable running up to a 'daughter' or 'slave' compass beside the steering wheel. Above the steering wheel one can see two identical sets of engine telegraphs. The boxes with the spoon-like locking levers in the background contain fuses, which tended to blow too frequently during action when upset by nearby explosions.

The development phases of the smaller, more agile boat are most fascinating and the result, *Vesikko*, represents a significant milestone in submarine history. It was developed from the successful German First World War Type UB II and was further improved to become the Type II of the Second World War. Yet, despite such a comparatively long history, it started life not as a coastal defence boat but as a means of hitting the Russians in the back, by being capable of operating on Lake Lagoda, to the east of St. Petersburg. Although the Russians gave Finland its independence in 1918, there were enough influential voices calling to claw the newly-formed country back under the Russian yoke and the fires of the First World War were still smouldering when Finnish naval leaders turned to Germany to help in providing a repelling sting. Progress was slow and exceedingly jerky, so it was the summer of 1930 before the result was finally launched in Helsinki with the name of *Saukko*. This had a displacement of 99 tons, meaning it could carry only two small-calibre (45cm) torpedo tubes and had no room for any reloads. (These smaller torpedoes were originally developed for aircraft.) The interior of *Saukko* was so cramped that the torpedoes had to be loaded from the outside and the cradle for this laborious task was later improved for the revolutionary German Type XXIII electro-boat. *Saukko* had a length of about 33m and a surface range of 500nm at 8kt, an underwater range of 50nm at 4kt and a crew of 13. One contributing factor for choosing this relatively small size was that it could be cut into sections and transported by railway, if it needed to be moved a long way from its base.

The seeds for *Vesikko* were sown in April 1926 long before *Saukko* was launched and at a time when negotiations for *Saukko* were nowhere near complete. Karl Bartenbach, who commanded the German submarine school around the beginning of the war and later became Flag Officer for U-boats in Flanders, convinced the leaders of the Finnish Navy that the small boat did not have enough hitting power and would be of little use in serious combat. He pointed out that the first German UB I boats could not claim any great successes and the basic design would need to accommodate at least a couple of larger torpedoes with a diameter of 53cm. This extra weight made it necessary to double the size of the hull and, ideally, even make it a fraction bigger with a displacement of about 250 tons. The Germans also promised to provide the Finns with a new fast-running diesel engine. This was a revolutionary innovation for the time, capable of producing 350hp from an engine no larger than older, slower ones. This meant that German engineers had succeeded in doubling the output without increasing the size of the engine.

The depth-keeping or hydroplane controls were similar to those used during the First World War and this basic setup hardly changed by the Second World War, except that the majority of boats could then rely on power-assisted machinery. In fact it was so efficient that many post-war Federal German submarines also used a similar system, although by then power-assisted controls dominated.

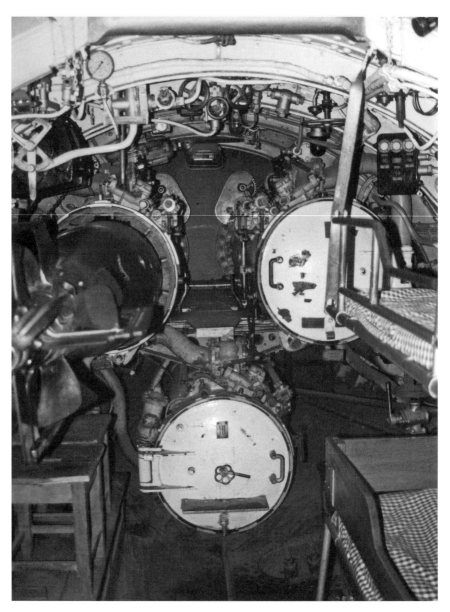

The torpedo department required virtually all the space from the conning tower to the bows and even then there was not enough room to load torpedoes forwards into the tubes. On Type II U-boats the loading hatch pointed backwards so that torpedoes could be reversed in, levelled out and then pushed forwards into the tubes. There was only enough space to carry two spares. It was possible to cram a third in, but that was usually prohibited because it created some serious stability problems and left hardly any room for the crew.

As additional bait, the Development Bureau had another fantastic carrot: the boat could be built in less than six months. This was so attractive to the newly-formed German Reichsmarine that its chief, Admiral Erich Raeder, produced an appealing financial package to push the Finns into accepting the proposal to build this new type of submarine. This is rather strange because Raeder, who was appointed as Commander-in-Chief of the German Navy in October 1928, was no great fan of underwater boats. Despite the short building time, *Vesikko* went through a very protracted development phase. The order was placed in 1931 but the boat was not launched until 10 May 1933. Following that it was tested by German personnel and not handed over to the Finnish navy until January 1936.

Vesikko's First World War predecessors had an exceptionally quick diving time of 30 seconds and stood up exceptionally well to depth-charging, a mode of attack which had been developed only during the last months of the First World War. So, in all the Germans were offering an attractive package, both mechanically and financially. Yet it turned out that the result was not without a multitude of serious hiccups. The valves in the main diving tanks were too small, meaning it took almost a whole minute for the boat to dive and its agility to cope with depth charges meant it was also exceedingly uncomfortable in rough weather. This was so bad that the accommodation in the rear could often not be used once the waves became too violent. Yet, under calmer conditions the engines did live up to their expectations and provided the boat with a good, reliable push. The problem was that they were also rather thirsty. The range of the Type UB II from 1915 of over 3,500nm at 8kt was reduced to less than 2,000nm and, on top of this, they were so noisy that it was virtually impossible to hold a conversation anywhere in the boat while the diesel engines were running. Although this was a nuisance, no one appeared to have been especially perturbed and much of the attention focused on the underwater handling qualities. For this it was fitted with two periscopes. One with a small head lens terminated inside the conning tower and a bigger, navigation periscope could be used from the central control room in the main pressure hull. As a weight and space-saving measure, the two were provided with only one motor and it was necessary to hitch up the right tube to the winding mechanism for raising and lowering it. Underwater steering was excellent, but depth keeping was more of a problem. Technology had advanced far enough by 1933 to balance (or trim) a boat so delicately that it would hardly go up or down once submerged. Yet, despite a sophisticated system of tanks and knowing that such a state of equilibrium is impossible to

Looking forwards towards the steering position with a thin bulkhead separating the central control room from the front section. On the left is the trimming panel that only the engineer officer and a few specially-trained men were allowed to operate when balancing the submerged boat to make it sit properly in the water. The partly-extended periscope hides the ladder leading up into the conning tower. (The commander would usually use the periscopes from the conning tower control room rather than the central control room.)

achieve, the diving characteristics were most disappointing. Valuable electricity had to be used to keep the motors running at some pace so that the depth rudders or hydroplanes could maintain a steady depth. Keeping the boat submerged at slow speeds while waiting for a target to approach was very difficult and could only be achieved by everybody remaining rooted to their spot and using a few men as mobile ballast. Controlling the depth at slow speeds became quite a challenge and an obvious field, which required much more research before the designers could provide a better and more foolproof system.

Despite these problems, *Vesikko* saw some service during the Second World War, attacking several ships and even sinking one of them. The boat was robust enough to go to sea during the cold winter months, but for most of the time was prevented from leaving the immediate coastal waters because the Germans had established a massive mine barrage

The diesel compartment of *Vesikko*. This is a modification of a First World War design with what was a revolutionary new type of diesel engine that produced the same power as an earlier one of almost twice its size. Yet despite the advance with such engines, there is very little to indicate the age of this photo and one would be forgiven if one thought this is a more modern Type II submarine.

across the Gulf of Finland to stop Soviet ships from leaving the eastern Baltic. The boat was decommissioned after the war and put up for sale, but seems not to have found a buyer, which made it possible for its former crew to restore it and set it up as a museum in Suomenlinna (Helsinki).

b. *Dekabrist* Class (*D-2*) in St. Petersburg

The first Russian submarines to be laid down after the First World War belonged to the *Dekabrist* or 'D' class, which were built in St. Petersburg (then Leningrad) on the Baltic and in Nikolayev on the Black Sea. This is significant because it was the first time that the Russians started

D-2 was about four times as heavy as *Vesikko*, but still lacked many of the modern power-assisted controls that played such an important role during the Second World War. Using muscle power to operate a boat the size of *Vesikko* must have required considerable tenacity, but struggling with something as big as *D-2* must have been highly exhausting work. The technology had advanced enough to make the main controls non-reversible by including a strong set of worm gears in the assembly. This meant that wind, currents or other heavy loads pressing against the outside blades could not move the controls in the wrong direction and the operators only needed their muscle power to move the machinery, not to hold it in place. This was a major problem with earlier sailing ships where half a dozen or more men were required to hold the steering wheel in rough weather.

building submarines on their own without direct foreign technological support, although there are suggestions that Turkish or Italian plans were used. On entering the museum boat in St. Petersburg one will immediately notice that it is virtually identical to the German Type IX. So, claims that the Russians used German plans from the First World War are almost certainly correct and it seems highly likely that German engineers helped with the development. The interesting point about *D-2* is that this class was launched in 1927–9 and therefore it gives an incredible insight into the technology of a period when muscle power was still very much the order of the day and motorised assistance, such as powered steering, was still in its infancy. *D-2* has a displacement of about 1,000 tons, making it four times as big as *Vesikko* and about the same size as the German Type IX. Controlling such a bulk at sea cannot have been easy without power-assisted machinery.

Some sources say that this class proved to be good and sturdy while others claim that the boats had considerable instability problems. The main hurdle with the technology was that the building process was nowhere near smooth and we are told that by the time the first boats were launched they were already some years behind those from other nations. Yet, they had some highly advanced features such as retractable forward hydroplanes, which must have been useful when it came to coping with ice in northern waters. It has also been said that these boats would hardly have met the demands put on them towards the end of the First World War, never mind having to cope with any future conflict. Yet amazingly they did see action during the Second World War and remained in service until many years after it.

A model of *D-2*'s sister-boat *D-3* on display at the International Maritime Museum of Hamburg (Germany).

Above, below and opposite: D-2 now set up as museum in St. Petersburg (formerly Leningrad). Although a little out of the way, it is easy to reach by public transport from the city centre. The site is small, making it difficult to photograph from the outside, but the inside is incredible with a generous and most helpful staff. On entering it quickly become apparent that this boat has all the important features of an early version of the German Type IX but without power-assisted controls.

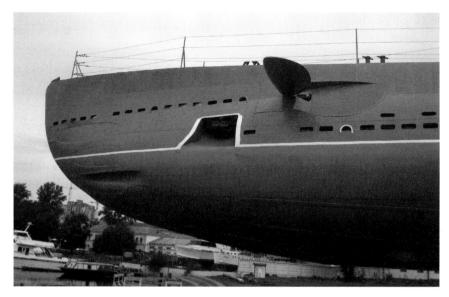

Two 'D' class boats were lost during trials shortly after launching (*Bezbozhnik* in September 1927 and *Krasnogvardeyetz* in June 1935). This may sound dramatic, but was nothing much out of the ordinary. Other nations suffered similar losses. One can blame such accidental sinkings on technology being so new that fail-safe systems had not yet made an appearance. So, it wasn't difficult for any crew of the time to accidentally sink their own submarine.

The *D-2* Museum in St. Petersburg is astonishing inasmuch that it is in brilliant condition and a considerable effort has been made to bring the human element back to life. Unlike many other museums, the batteries from the lower deck have been removed to use this comparatively large space for breathing the spirit of the past into the lifeless mechanics above. This effort really does bring home the fact that the boat was once filled with the energy of people and it is not difficult to see that those men who manned her had the same aspirations and desires as every other person on the planet. It was only their uniforms which made them different from submariners on the other side of the world; otherwise they appeared to have belonged to the same family. The condition of the interior is also remarkably good and so clean that it looks as if the crew has only just vacated it. *D-2* is indeed a remarkable reminder of the past and it is fantastic that this boat has been preserved in such brilliant condition, by a most obliging team.

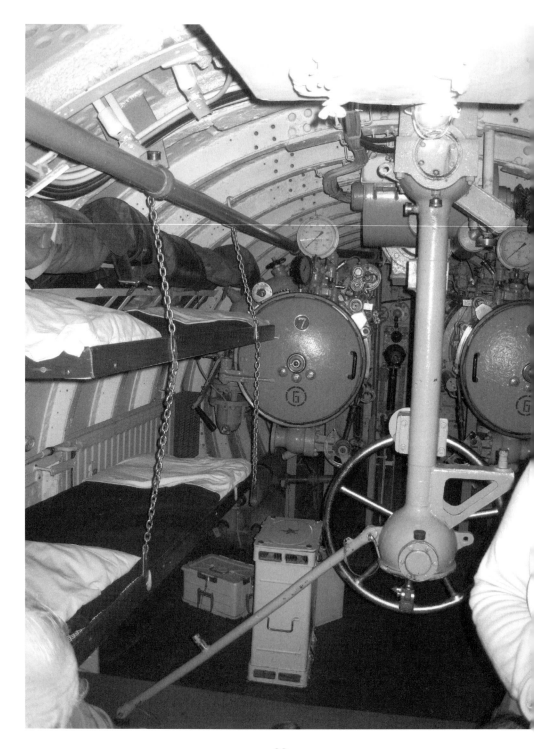

EARLY DEVELOPMENTS

The diesel engine compartment. Try to find a clue that this photograph was not taken inside a Second World War submarine. This shows how much progress had been made with these engines in the quarter of a century since Rudolf Diesel had invented them. Yet, outward appearances can be most deceptive because many engines were improved considerably by adding boosters and superchargers to give them a considerably higher output than earlier models with the same appearance.

Opposite: The stern torpedo tubes with the emergency steering wheel in operational position. Trying to date the technology in this picture is exceedingly difficult and people would be forgiven if they think that this boat came from the Second World War or even from the post-war era. Everything is in magnificent condition.

Above: The impressive bow torpedo compartment. One wonders what might have happened during the Second World War if U-boats had attacked convoys with such heavy armament. During the autumn of 1940 and again during the initial attack against the United States successes were often muted because U-boat aces were forced to withdraw to reload torpedoes and then had problems finding their targets again. With *D-2*'s armament the long-distance Type IX boats could have shot a total of eight instead of six torpedoes while the Type VIIs had only five. The cleanliness of this museum is incredible with people putting in a lot of effort to keep the machinery in such prime condition. Even the floor looks clean enough to eat off at mid-day after many people had already trampled over it.

Opposite above: These hydroplane controls help to date the mechanics in the *D-2* museum. The knobs on the hand wheels suggest that the men operating them must have needed considerable grip with high muscle power to work this cumbersome machinery.

Opposite below: One of the pressure-resisting bulkheads inside *D-2*.

EARLY DEVELOPMENTS

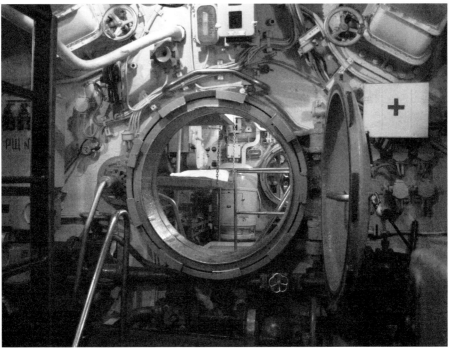

HITLER'S ATTACK U-BOATS

The periscope with hydroplane controls beyond.

Finding the heads is always useful for non-submariners because it is easy to guess its purpose.

Chapter 5

The Second World War in a Nutshell

History books tell us that Germany had an advantage at the beginning of the Second World War because her submarines were modern, while other navies were still nurturing old and often obsolete models. However, after analysing basic facts one must come to a totally different conclusion.

First, when considering submarine development it is necessary to bear the timescale in mind. There were only twelve and eight years respectively from the British *Holland 1* and the German *U 1* until the beginning of the First World War; not much time for producing an entirely new weapon. The following four war years were chaotic, where designers were constantly forced to meet new demands from the fronts, often without being able to evaluate their results properly. Following the end of the First World War there were only two decades until the beginning of the Second and Germany had not been allowed to build or own submarines for the first seventeen years of that short period. So the U-boat arm of the Second World War was only a little over four years old when the war started.

Despite a considerable new U-boat build-up in Germany from 1935 onwards, other nations appear to have considered the future uses of submarines far more thoroughly than the Germans, whose main attacking armament was based on one heavy gun and a maximum of four bow torpedo tubes. Other countries were thinking along the lines of six bow tubes plus two in the stern. One reason for this was that submarines were expected to be attacking from such considerable distances that they needed to fire a salvo of two or three torpedoes to get one hit. Britain's bigger boats had eight and the large *Triton* class even ten torpedo tubes. So, the main armament of German U-boats was considerably weaker than equivalent boats in other navies and many of the other main features were also significantly inferior. For example, German U-boats were without a ventilation system, there was no venting system for the batteries, no fitted system for the removal of carbon dioxide from the air and no way of replenishing used oxygen. (Batteries gave off hydrogen and oxygen when charging and discharging, and this highly explosive mixture was vented into the interior of the boat – while is why naked flames were not permitted and men were not allowed to smoke inside the submarine.) German U-boats had only one practical heads (lavatory) for fifty men and this could not be used once the boat dived deep. The high-pressure heads for deep diving was not introduced until after U-boats had lost their grip on the convoy battles in the Atlantic. The larger boats had two heads, but one was usually used for food storage. There were no provisions for the men to wash themselves or their clothing, no adequate food storage facilities and the insides of all boats were exceedingly cramped. The galley was small, hardly adequate to cater for so many men, many of the controls were hand operated with little or no automation and so the list goes on.

When the British captured *U-570* (Kapitänleutnant Hans-Joachim Rahmlow) in the summer of 1942 it was discovered that the reason why the crew had experienced so many mechanical failures was due to switches having jumped to the 'off' position on their own. This was especially troublesome because the majority of controls were definitely still 'hand operated', without any form of automation or of locking them into the desired position. The Royal Navy also noted that an inexperienced crew could easily operate the controls and the Type VIIC could dive deeper than the maximum settings on British depth charges. Despite these advantages, many men remarked that the endurance as well as the living and the fighting conditions were inferior to British submarines and British boats were already inferior to those of the United States.

The big problem with the new detection device, Asdic, was that it worked only when the target was submerged and it could not detect surfaced U-boats. The German U-boat onslaught against British merchant ships during the autumn of 1940 was so successful because the attacks were made on the surface at night and from such close range that a single torpedo would sink a ship, if it functioned properly. Surfaced submarines were difficult and often impossible to spot in the darkness of the night, thus they were in a good position to decimate

Allied merchant shipping. The dreadful torpedo failures, which made such significant contribution to the outcome of the battle, have been described in other books and are beyond the scope of this work.

Another significant milestone followed when the carnage in the shipping lanes stopped abruptly and most dramatically during December 1940 and March 1941. When looking at the statistics one can see that since the summer of 1940 each U-boat at sea had been sinking up to six merchant ships per month and this dropped to less than three during the first months of 1941. To make matters worse, this downward trend continued until the end of the war. So what caused this rapid decline? The weather must have played a significant role, but what other gremlins were active at the time?

March 1941 is easier to explain. It was the period when the new invention of radar had its first success against surfaced U-boats. Radar could 'see' U-boats as they closed in on their prey. So the supreme advantage of autumn 1940 when U-boats attacked from close range on the surface at night was lost. This was made even worse for the Germans by another British development; the high frequency radio direction finder (H/F D/F or 'Huff Duff'), which indicated the direction from which even exceedingly short messages were coming from. U-boats tended to maintain radio silence until just before an attack, when they started flooding the ether with masses of signals. Thus, such direction finders installed in escorts and merchant ships warned of an impending attack and gave the escort commander enough time to employ his limited resources to cut off the incoming U-boats. Radar was used to locate them on the surface and, once driven under, Asdic made it possible to place depth charges most effectively. This combination appeared for the first time during the summer of 1941 and by October H/F D/F had been fitted to many escorts and merchant ships, providing them with a supreme advantage. What is more, Germany did not become aware of H/F D/F until the very end of the war, providing the Allies with an incredibly useful aid that was to play 'the' most significant role in the war at sea. It is strange that no one on the German side seems to have noticed the vast H/F D/F aerials high up on the tallest part of the ships' superstructures.

For much of the war, Britain could also read the U-boat radio code; so anti-submarine forces could be deployed in the most profitable areas. It is important to add that U-boat sinkings did not rise dramatically as a result of these new introductions because Britain did not have sufficient escorts to hunt them to extinction. Instead, escort commanders were told to force U-boats under, so that they lost contact with the convoy, and then return as quickly as possible to their protective position around the merchant ships. This was so effective that it was possible keep the majority of U-boats far enough away to prevent them from launching attacks. But this effectiveness is very much hidden by the propaganda of the period that still wants us to believe Britain was on the brink of disaster by being cut off by U-boats. Yet, looking at the statistics one can see that the number of U-boats at sea throughout 1942 had increased significantly to reach a hundred by the end of the summer and remained at that high level for almost a whole year until May 1943. Despite these huge numbers, the first clash of Titans, when two convoys ran into the teeth of a large wolf pack, did not take place until March 1943 and in 1942 the majority of U-boats came home without having seen a single target.

Towards the autumn of 1941, that is after two years of war, it was becoming obvious to German leaders that Britain was gaining the upper hand in the convoy war and new plans had to be made to cope with the increasingly serious threat from the air. Improved anti-aircraft guns were installed, but these proved ineffective against modern, fast-flying and armoured aircraft. By the following autumn it was blatantly obvious that the existing U-boats had come to the end of their effective life and a totally new type was required.

Such an idea of producing a new type of submarine was by no means new; it had been suggested before Hitler's regime was allowed to build submarines, but so little research was carried out that it would to be a while before any of this technology could be mass produced. This meant that stopgap measures were going to be essential from the summer and autumn of 1942 onwards, to prevent Germany losing its entire submarine fleet to aircraft. To meet these new demands the large gun in front of the conning tower was removed so that the heavy weight could be replaced with increased anti-aircraft guns on platforms behind the tower. Up to that period of time the majority of U-boats had been fitted with one single-barrelled 20mm anti-aircraft gun. The platform it was mounted on was made bigger to accommodate two twin versions of these and another platform was added a little lower down to hold a single 37mm semi-automatic weapon. However, these were in such short supply that many boats carried a quadruple 20mm gun instead. Both these combinations proved to be ineffective against modern aircraft and a more effective twin 37mm was provided for larger boats shortly before the end of the war. In most cases the rule of thumb that the 37mm were fitted to Type IX boats and the 20mm quadruple to Type VIIs seems to hold fast, although there were some of this type with 37mm guns.

Towards the end of the war some U-boats were modified to carry a breathing pipe or schnorkel, so that the diesel engines could be run without having to surface. These were not really successful and only made the difference between death and marginal survival. There was no way that schnorkels could put U-boats back onto the offensive. To tackle convoys, Germany needed a totally new type of submarine, one that the world had not seen before. The high-speed experimental craft were nowhere near ready for mass production and a stopgap measure had to be introduced. This was the so-called electro-submarine, capable of high underwater speeds and without having to surface to charge its batteries. Two types were constructed, the small coastal Type XXIII and the larger ocean-going Type XXI. None of the smaller type have survived, but a larger one exists as a museum in Bremerhaven with the name of *Wilhelm Bauer*. They were revolutionary inasmuch that prefabricated sections, often built far inland, were transported to the shipyards for final assembly. Once in the water these boats were capable of diving down to 200m and moving at almost 17 knots, faster than the majority of ships sent out to hunt them. This speed was achieved by merely having a large hull filled with many more batteries than existing boats could carry. Yet almost all the technology in these boats had been around in 1935, but at that time no one was interested in building a submarine with high underwater speed.

Chapter 6

1935: The New Generation of Attack U-boats

a. Type II

The last foreign soldiers of the army of occupation left Germany in July 1930, less than three years before Hitler came to power. They had been stationed in Germany to assure that war reparations were paid and they

A model of a Type IID U-boat on display in the International Maritime Museum of Hamburg (Germany) showing many of the common features. The majority of these small coastal boats were used for training in the eastern Baltic, where they were out of reach of enemy forces. Only a few of the more advanced versions saw service in the Atlantic, where they made a significant contribution by hitting at shipping. In addition to this, a good number of the so-called ace commanders saw their first action in these small boats. It was a Type IIC, *U-57* under Kapitänleutnant Erich Topp, that launched the first short-range surface attack at night, hitting three ships on 24 August 1940 with three separately-aimed torpedoes that were all fired within a couple of minutes of each other (*Saint Dunstan* and *Cumberland* were sunk while the third, *Havildar*, was damaged but reached port).

did not shy away from using their guns against starving Germans who could only watch when the food and goods they had produced were taken away. In view of this cruelty, it was thought highly likely that this army of occupation would return, to confiscate any military violations of the Versailles 'Treaty', the peace 'treaty' that the Germans were forced to sign at the end of the First World War. So, there was no point in putting the latest technology into the new submarines that were being secretly built at Deutsche Werke in Kiel. As it happened, the victorious Allies did not send in another army of occupation. Instead, in March 1935, when Hitler repudiated what he called the 'Betrayal' of Versailles, they applauded and offered him the most generous terms in the Anglo-German Naval Agreement. This allowed the Germany to build their submarine strength up to one-third of the British Royal Navy's tonnage, with an additional clause to increase this if they sacrificed tonnage in other categories of ship.

The hardly usable Type IIA was quickly improved to such an extent that the later versions saw action in the Atlantic, but the boats were too small to go far from their bases and most of them remained in the eastern Baltic for training. Yet these 'North Sea Ducks' played a significant role inasmuch that many of the early aces gained their initial experience in them. It is also important to remember that the first of the highly effective short-range surface attacks at night was launched during the autumn of 1940 by one of these tiny boats (*U-57* under Erich Topp).

b. Type VII

Although the small Type II coastal boats were the first to be launched by the National Socialists, it was the larger Type I that formed the core of the already existing covert planning process. The Anglo-German Naval Agreement, signed in June 1935, thwarted this planning and instead of developing a series of specialised craft, the German High Command changed direction to concentrate on general-purpose vessels in order to comply with the new tonnage limitations. At the same time Germany switched over to develop the Type VII instead of the Type I, of which only two boats were ever produced. Although the Type VII became the largest class of submarine to have been built, only one (*U-995*) survives as a museum. This is situated beside the Naval Memorial at Laboe near Kiel.

U-995 served in the Norwegian Navy after the Second World War and was modified for this new role. Once decommissioned in 1958, it was

1935: THE NEW GENERATION OF ATTACK U-BOATS

U-32, a Type VIIA with the external rear torpedo tube just visible at the stern. The vents along the sides varied considerably from later versions and the saddle tanks are hardly visible, although they were already an important feature under the cladding.

handed back to Germany and re-built to resemble its 1945 appearance. Unfortunately there were no longer any navigation periscopes from the early period and *U-995* was fitted with two standard attack periscopes. These had a considerably smaller head lenses than the other type. Once the boat was in-situ in what is a public place, there were many attempts to steal from it and souvenir hunters came with a good selection of tools. One night someone even removed the radio direction finder from the top of the conning tower. Sadly there were no replacements and a new loop was built with a much thinner ring than the original. The interesting point is that this false piece of equipment has since featured in many films as a representative of the real item. The interior of the boat suffered in a similar fashion and many parts have been unscrewed and removed by thieves. Only a few items could be replaced with authentic equipment. So, sadly, parts of the boat now look a little depleted. Removing items from submarines is dead easy because everything was designed so that it could be taken to pieces for repairing at sea.

The Type VII had roots going back to the dark days of the First World War, when UB class submarines were being developed under

challenging wartime conditions. The basic concepts were further modified after the war, when the secret German Development Bureau in Holland helped with the building the *Vetehinen* class in Finland. The Type VII became known as the VIIA and a modified version, the VIIB, was added to the stocks before the first VIIA had been launched. One major reason for this modification was that the Type VIIA did not have a stern torpedo tube inside the pressure hull but rather an external one, located above the pressure hull where the crew could not access it once the boat was at sea. This meant it was impossible to carry the newer electric torpedo (G7e) because this needed to be removed from its tube at least once every three days to recharge the batteries.

The other torpedo, the G7a, with an internal combustion engine, was faster, but distilled water was injected into its engine to make steam and this froze solid during the German winters, meaning the submarine would be without a sting in its tail for several cold months. Removing the single rudder so that the new, exceedingly heavy internal torpedo tube could be placed along the central axis of the boat solved the problem. Two rudders working in tandem were then added, one on each side of the outside door. This setup worked well, although between twelve and twenty boats were without a stern tube and a handful had them welded shut as the result of battle damage.

Individual fittings inside the boats as well as the thickness of the pressure hull were constantly improved and these modifications gave rise to the Type VIIC and later the Type VIIC/41. *U-995* is an example of this Type VIIC/41 version. Further improvements were planned as well but none of the Type VIIC/42 were ever built. One of the many strange points in this development was that no one tried any long runs with the early Type VII boats. It was not until the beginning of 1942, after the United States had joined in the war, that the seagoing Type VII was

Opposite: U-73, showing the main deck features of a Type VIIB. The bulge around the gun, to allow the crew easier access, varied and in some cases the side walls bulged outwards to follow the edge of the enlarged platform rather than run underneath it, as in this photograph. The lid of the ready-use ammunition container for the 88mm gun can be seen forward, towards the right near the mooring rope where a docking fender is lying on the deck. Synthetic ropes were not invented until long after the war and it was common to take such organic material below so that it could dry out in the engine room to prevent it from rotting. The saddle tank containing negative buoyancy and regulatory bunkers and other cells is clearly visible along the waterline.

Left and below: U-172, an ocean-going Type IXC, with a radar aerial attached to the front of the conning tower.

found to be capable of crossing the Atlantic. Boats making their way to Canada discovered that their range turned out to have been much greater than the navy had originally anticipated.

U-995, launched in July 1943, represents the latest development of this Type VII class, but it was only marginally better than its predecessor which fired the first torpedoes of the war. The pressure hull was thicker and stronger to cope with depth charges, the controls were safer and easier to handle and there were all manner of other minor modifications as a result of war experience, but none of them made this a revolutionary submarine. In fact it wasn't even adequate for keeping up with the times.

It had already been learned during the First World War that rigid mountings for machinery in submarines were useless because they tended to snap under the slightest provocation when depth charges rattled the boat. Therefore many parts were joined with

A plastic model on display at the German U-boat Museum in Cuxhaven-Altenbruch showing the later arrangement of vents along the side of a Type VIIC with additional anti-aircraft armament that was added after the beginning of 1942. There used to be some truly appalling models for self-assembly, but in recent years manufacturers have produced some excellent kits with more accurate features. Here the top lip of the conning tower looks very much like the earlier version, which would have been altered by the time the heavy anti-aircraft armament was added, and it is likely that these Type VIIC boats would have had a quadruple 20mm on the lower platform instead of the larger single 37mm. Type VII boats had a comparatively narrow upper deck with a noticeable bulge forward of the conning tower where the 88mm gun was located. The other main feature, which this class shared with the later Type II boats, is the set of noticeable saddle tanks along the sides of the central section.

German pressure hulls were usually circular rather than oval and sometimes constructed in sections away from the main slips. This speeded up the building process by reducing the time needed in those hard-pressed areas near the water's edge.

flexible connections to prevent a severe shaking from breaking them. The first Type VII boats found, among other things, that this principle had been applied a little too liberally. The main engines vibrated free from their base plates when running at high speeds for prolonged periods, meaning major modifications were necessary.

1935: THE NEW GENERATION OF ATTACK U-BOATS

U-357 (Type VIIC) showing the fairing or casing that has been added to the top of the circular pressure hull so that men could work on the upper deck especially when docking or using the gun. The so-called saddle tanks are clearly visible on both sides near the conning tower.

U-93 under Claus Korth. Emblem enthusiasts could be excused if they thought this shows the 'Red Devil' boat *U-552* under Erich Topp, but the first version of this emblem appeared on *U-57* while this small Type II was under the command of Korth, who was succeeded by Topp. Korth took the emblem with him to his new command *U-93*, one of the early Type VIIC boats built at the Germania Works in Kiel. Note how the side of the hull curves around the outside of the bulge around the deck gun, instead of running underneath it as can be seen in other photographs. The bulge at the forward base of the conning tower contains a magnetic compass that was viewed by the helmsman down below in the central control room through an illuminated periscope. The 'D'-shaped deck cover above the galley hatch can be seen sticking up behind the conning tower.

What is so astonishing is that the Type VII remained in production long after it had been found to be obsolete and the new Type XXI electro-boats were already in production. Over 600 Type VII boats were put onto the stocks, making this the most numerous class of submarine ever built. This figure is slightly misleading because a total of 1,171 U-boats were commissioned during the Second World War, but less than 350 of them came into contact with the enemy. Some 850 boats never came within shooting distance of a target. School boats, supply tankers, experimental craft and so forth were never in a position to attack anything, but despite this there appears to be an incredibly large number of U-boats which didn't contribute a great deal to the war.

c. Type IX

The Type IX differed from the Type VII by having a double hull with tanks wrapped around the outside of the pressure hull. This also had roots going back to the First World War, having been based on the *U-81* type from that period. The designers were looking for a long-range, ocean-going boat and, at the same time, one big enough to accommodate a flotilla leader with his staff. The original specification for 'long range' was to reach possible hotspots in the eastern Mediterranean, operate there for some time and then return to Germany without refuelling.

Although history books tell us that wolf packs were an invention of the Second World War, group attacks had already taken place. Most of them were defeated by technology, such as radios not being efficient enough to get the boats to the right place at the right time.

The double hull of the Type IX made it possible to add a considerably wider deck than that fitted on the smaller Type VII and the larger size made it possible to carry more weight up top. This shows the typically wide deck of the Type IX.

It was envisaged that U-boats of the future would operate as small flotillas, similar to the newly-emerging motor torpedo boats, rather than individually. Having the commander of such a group, together with his staff of half a dozen or so, on board meant the boat needed additional communications equipment. The volume of messages to be transmitted would be greater, so more men would be needed to work the radios.

The initial design of the Type IX must have been pretty good because there were hardly any complaints and only minor modifications were added later. These came about as a result of suggestions from men who took these larger boats to Spain, where they served as part of an international peacekeeping force during the Civil War. Some boats that were secretly in those waters penetrated some way into the Mediterranean, yet 'long range' in those days was still not terribly far. Once the war broke out they were expected to go even further, to West Africa and later on to Cape Town.

The biggest problem came when Japan and the United States joined in the war and it became desirable to have some very-long-range boats, capable of not just crossing the Atlantic to the eastern seaboard of the United States, but going as far as the Indian Ocean and perhaps even to Japan. Surface supply ships were no longer viable. Almost all had

A Type IXC/40 with the special bow modification to make the boat dive faster than those with wider bows. This shows a model by Detlef Simon.

1935: THE NEW GENERATION OF ATTACK U-BOATS

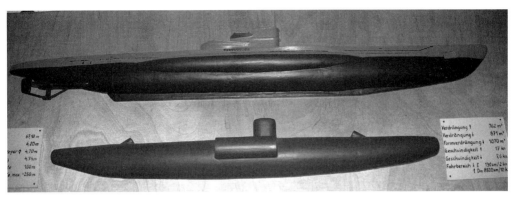

A simple three-dimensional diagram on display at the German U-boat Museum in Cuxhaven-Altenbruch showing the pressure hull at the bottom and the complete boat with its streamlined casing on the top. The Type IX had a similar set-up with identical tanks along the side, but these were incorporated into the double hull and therefore they are not visible as noticeable bulges.

been hunted to extinction. This meant that any new very-long-range U-boat would have to manage it on its own and there was no way that an ordinary Type IXC could cover such enormous distances. The big problem was finding a suitable engine, one that would use the minimum of fuel. Such power plants did exist, but they were not powerful enough to chase after fast-moving targets. So, in the end, it was decided to fit both into the boat. This meant lengthening the rear section to accommodate the extra machinery. Of course, such an addition put the rest out of equilibrium and another accommodation section was added in the front to balance the new design. The bottom part of the accommodation area was filled with batteries, which were heavy enough to counterbalance the additional weight aft of the periscopes. All this provided massive space for fuel bunkers in the tanks around the outside of the pressure hull, giving this new type an enormous range of more than 32,000nm, twice as much as a Type IXC. Two of these boats were developed without armament as the Type IXD1 before production began with the fighting version of the Type IXD2. Sadly, none of these very-long-range boats survive.

The main problem with the Type IXCs was that they were not as agile as the smaller Type VIICs and they were slower in diving, which became critical when attacked by fast-flying aircraft. The other problem was that the outer skin was a comparatively thin coat of tanks wrapped around the strong pressure hull, meaning it was more susceptible to depth-charge damage. Yet the Type IXC proved to be an excellent

There was enough space between the pressure hull and the upper (outside) deck for a man to crawl through on all fours. This space was used to accommodate a variety of ducts, compressed air bottles, torpedo storage tubes, ammunition containers and so forth. Of course the vents along the sides and gaps in deck slats meant that this space filled with water every time the boat dived.

workhorse and a large number were produced. Almost fifty IXCs were commissioned and just over ninety IXC/40s. In addition to this there were two IXD1s and almost thirty IXD2s. The fourteen Type IXB boats were among the most successful of the war, sinking more ships than the majority of other types, and the most successful operational voyage in terms of tonnage sunk was when *U-107* operated in distant waters during the summer of 1942. The reason for this success was that these boats turned up unexpectedly in areas still without effective submarine hunters, so they faced comparatively little opposition.

Chapter 7

Attack U-boats: Their Main External Features

The Upper Deck

Individual external components such as hatches, vents along the sides and the arrangement of handrails were often left for individual yards to use their own patterns and patents. These differed sufficiently to provide a good aid for helping with the identification of photographs. Some of this early recognition work by the Swedish historian Lennart Lindberg has been published in the later Erich Gröner books and other interesting snippets have appeared in books by Fritz Köhl and Axel Niestlé, but there are considerably more notes from the U-boat engineer Christoph Aschmoneit in the German U-boat Museum. It would appear that much of this has not yet been published.

When using upper-deck features for identifying old photographs, it is important to bear in mind that the commander had to remain on the bridge as long as men were on deck. During the early years maintenance work was restricted to reasonably calm conditions, but when the war started it was necessary for men to be outside under rougher conditions and therefore many handrails were strengthened and additional handholds added. So it is possible to find photos of the same boats with different features. Despite these useful variations, many of the fittings were fairly similar and a general description of the external features should cover the main points.

So, starting at the bows, it will quickly become apparent that the only anchor was on the starboard (right-hand) side and photos of early boats often show a leftover from the First World War, when serrated net-cutters were thought to have been essential. Most of these had

U-42 (Type IXA) seen from *U-53* showing the protrusions on the bows of a Type VIIB. At the front one can see the jumping wire with insulators running down from the top of the conning tower to the net cutter. Moving towards the camera, there is a 'T'-shaped sound detector head covered with a canvas hood. This device rotated and the 'T' shape was hardly noticeable when looking at it sideways-on. The next item is the head of the capstan. This was usually removed when not required and therefore does not feature in many photographs. Nearer the camera is a red and white rescue buoy with light bulb on top that could be released by the crew in an emergency. These were removed at the beginning of the war to prevent depth charges from blowing them out of their holders and thereby automatically engaging the flashing light. In the foreground on the right and flush with the deck one can make out the circular tops of the mooring bollards that could be lifted up when required. Also note that the deck slats did not form a continuous deck along the bows, but were made up of several sections that hinged upwards. The railings, consisting of a plain steel cable on supports, were not permanently attached to the deck but merely screwed into position and usually removed at the end of the training period.

vanished by the time the Second World War started, but remained on some boats until at least the summer of 1940. Jumping wires running down from the top of the conning tower to the tops of these cutters were later attached to the deck. Right forward was an obvious hole with smooth edges. The idea was that towropes should be threaded through

ATTACK U-BOATS: THEIR MAIN EXTERNAL FEATURES

U-31 (Type VIIA), sunk by an aircraft in the Jade Estuary outside Wilhelmshaven in March 1940, is seen here after having been raised again. Note that the 'T'-shaped sound detector head has been replaced by the Group Listening Device, so-called because it consisted of a semicircular set (or group) of directional hydrophones located above the forward hydroplanes. A variety of different designs were introduced throughout the war.

it and then attached to a strong hook welded onto the pressure hull. This was not there so much as a help-you-home aid after a breakdown, but for towing boats through ice-infested coastal waters so that they didn't have to risk damaging their propellers.

Jumping wires were usually arranged so that a single cable ran from the top of the conning tower to the bows and a double set connected the gun platform with the stern. Later during the war there were a few boats with a double set of wires at the front so that these would not interfere with radar signals transmitted from the front of the conning tower. The thick wires were originally put there to prevent the conning tower from snagging when running under anti-submarine netting.

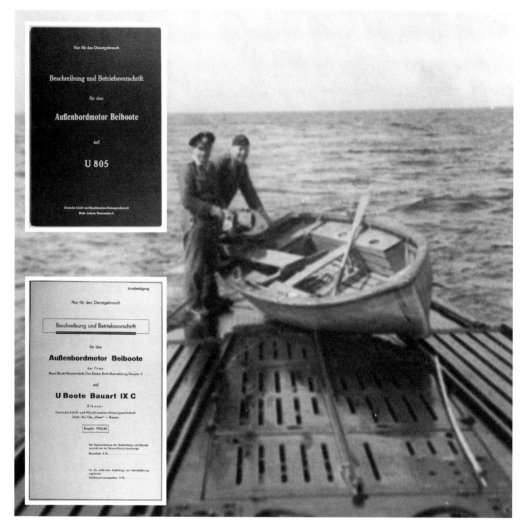

Type IX boats were large enough to carry a specially-built dinghy. These had a soft, often leather-padded top to lie upside down in their storage box. The wooden flotation compartments along the stern and sides are clearly visible in this rather poor photograph. Both the bottom of the hull and these wooden compartments had ventilation holes with screw-in caps that had to be inserted before the boat could be used. These allowed air into the boxes and hull and they filled with water when the submarine dived. These dinghies were not provided as an afterthought, but were a permanent part of the submarine's equipment and they had their own outboard engines with instruction manual. Yet there is very little reference that these boats were ever used during the war, even in situations where they would have provided a useful aid for hard-pressed crews.

ATTACK U-BOATS: THEIR MAIN EXTERNAL FEATURES

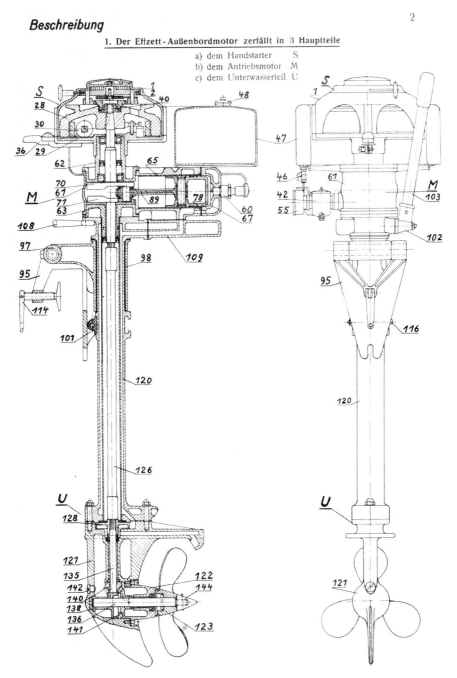

Above and opposite inset: The handbook from *U-805* (Type IXC/40) for using the outboard engine.

Although such actions feature frequently in films and novels, there were very few incidents of U-boats having to cope with such obstructions.

During the Second World War the wires served a twofold purpose. First, as radio aerials. It is often possible to see a number of round spherical lumps at both ends. These were insulators to prevent the middle part of the wire earthing or short-circuiting to the hull. Touching the wires while they were being used for this purpose would have resulted in an electric shock. When switched off, the wires doubled up as an attachment for safety harnesses to help men working on the upper deck.

The motor for raising the anchor could be declutched from the chain winding mechanism and a capstan attached on top. It would seem that these small capstans were made for a variety of different boats. They had sockets on the top so that long poles could be inserted for men to turn them when mechanical power failed. The main problem with this was that the deck was too narrow and there was no room for a group of men to carry out such arduous work. Some U-boat men have said that the capstan was hydraulic but there are also diagrams showing these driven by the anchor motor, so it is possible that two different types were produced.

The other feature was a 'T'-shaped stalk with underwater microphones called hydrophones for the sound detector. The stalk rotated and could give a fairly accurate indication of any noise source. This device was so sensitive that it could hear ships that were too far away for lookouts to see from the top of the conning tower. The so-called Group Listening Apparatus, that was located towards the bottom of the bows, later replaced them ('Group' because there was a set or group of several hydrophones pointing in different directions.)

Opposite: The Type VIIs (seen here) had one and Type IXs two torpedo storage tubes side-by-side in the bows and another set in the stern. Theoretically these were water and pressure-resistant containers, but they sometimes leaked so that boats in the Arctic could not withdraw the torpedo because the entire system had frozen into one solid lump. The gun was turned sideways so that the loading gear could be assembled to pull the torpedo out of the tube before being lowered through the normal hatch into the pressure hull. A well-trained crew could carry out this procedure in a little more than half an hour, but in many cases crews did not practise this often enough, so it took an hour or more and required considerable muscle power. There are several references in logbooks where commanders criticised the inefficiency of this system, saying something simpler would have helped. Note that there isn't much to prevent the men from falling overboard and that the hatch covers in the deck have been reinforced with diagonal supports.

ATTACK U-BOATS: THEIR MAIN EXTERNAL FEATURES

Every boat also had a double set of retractable twin mooring bollards, which were raised manually when they were required for docking. On most boats there was a double set along both sides, but some also had them in the centre of the deck.

When trimmed for quick diving, the top of the pressure hull was roughly level with the surface of the water and the space between this and the upper deck was large enough for a man to crawl through on all fours. The deck slats were made either out of teak or metal with a large number of gaps so that the space behind the side vents could quickly fill with water. Many years ago a veteran described the slats

U-515 showing the wider deck of a Type IXC with enough space to hold two torpedo storage tubes side by side. In this case the empty tube is being used to load cargo. Having sunk a ship the men found themselves surrounded with masses of floating butter crates. One man is using his feet to slide these valuable items into the storage tube.

The forward hydroplanes of a Type VIIC. Atlantic gales were strong enough to bend the supporting rods so much that the planes could not be fully rotated until repaired in port.

as having been made from best German oak, which appears to come from his imagination. No other person who served in U-boats had ever seen this, but several authors swallowed the mistake with great enthusiasm.

The space between the pressure hull and the upper deck slats contained a variety of features such as ventilation shafts, torpedo storage tubes and compressed-air bottles, most of which are not visible in photographs. The trapdoors above the main hatches were usually rectangular or 'D' shaped. In addition to these, photographs show other, slightly upward-bulging circular covers. At first these were the tops of water and pressure-resistant containers for small quantities of ready-use ammunition. More were added in later years for holding inflatable life rafts. Although these saved comparatively few lives, they were great morale boosters for the crew. There were no hard-and-fast rules about where any containers should be located and it is possible to find a good number of variations in photographs.

The stern of *U-534* (Type IXC/40) showing how the thick steel plating of the pressure hull was buckled so badly that it cracked, allowing water to pour in and sink the boat. The twin rudders, always working in tandem, and the hydroplanes were a weak link in the construction and liable to fail if depth charges came too close. Men from a modern propeller manufacturer in Birkenhead, watching the arrival of the U-boat long after the war, said that the propeller design of *U-534* was many years ahead of its time.

Some U-boats were also fitted with a storage container for holding a rowing boat. These were specially-designed wooden craft with floatation chambers, but usually so small that they could not accommodate more than three or four men. The naval command even designed a dedicated outboard motor for them. What is so strange that the navy never provided adequate craft for landing operations or for transferring goods between U-boats at sea, although it must have been known that carrying heavy provisions in boxes with sharp edges in rubber dinghies with soft floors was difficult or even impossible because the wooden crates often broke through the thin rubber. Boats detailed for landing operations found that rocks or gravel on beaches often damaged the bottoms of these craft, meaning that dedicated small boats with hard bottoms would have been a great help. In some cases the inflatables

ATTACK U-BOATS: THEIR MAIN EXTERNAL FEATURES

The stern of *U-995* at Laboe near Kiel (Germany). A navigation light is just visible on the top of the hull.

rubbed against the wall of their containers, scraping a hole in the rubber to render them useless before they were inflated.

Before the war U-boats were usually fitted with two red-and-white-striped rescue buoys, nicknamed *Spatz* (Sparrow). These had a light on top with a telephone and could be released from inside a crippled submarine. The snag was that when blown out of their seating by a depth charge the light would automatically start flashing and therefore the bulbs were removed on the eve of war and the rest of the device was dismantled shortly afterwards. They only tend to feature in pre-war photographs and on some training boats that didn't make it as far as the front.

Guns

It was the Second Watch Officer, the one with the least experience and the easiest to replace if he fell overboard, who was responsible for climbing about on the upper deck to deal with the guns. Towards the beginning of the war there were strict rules that the vulnerable moving parts had to be serviced each day to assure that everything was functioning properly and while this was done, there was another routine to check that the barrels were free from obstructions. It was common for each watch to have its own gun crew, but these men did not always have to be on duty on top of the conning tower. The crew for the large deck guns often did not put in an appearance at all and their duties ended with checking that the ready-use ammunition was where it should be. They also checked that explosive and incendiary shells were available in the correct proportions as ordered by the commander. Anti-aircraft guns were usually test-fired at the beginning of each day, the magazines made ready and the men would then be stood down if the boat was in an aircraft-free area. After capturing *U-570* in mid-Atlantic on 27 August 1941, a Royal Navy officer remarked that it was unusual for U-boats to carry a complete set of spares, including barrels for their anti-aircraft guns, and he added that the one on *U-570* worked extremely well.

U-20 (Type IIB) showing the early conning tower arrangement with the attack periscope with the small head lens raised a little towards the right of the men on the bridge. Type II boats were too small to carry heavy guns and most of them were fitted only with one small 20mm weapon. These sat on a variety of different mounts. The common variety, a circular tower mount, is seen here. The object on the deck behind it is a docking fender.

ATTACK U-BOATS: THEIR MAIN EXTERNAL FEATURES

Above and right: Not brilliant photographs, but they show how the 20mm anti-aircraft was aimed and fired.

An 88mm gun with watertight tampion screwed in position. Both gun sights on the left and right are in position and light from the bright sky is shining through the optics to produce the white circles. The brackets for supporting the gunners have been turned outwards in the operating position and these would normally be reversed when the gun was not in use to make more space on deck. One of the hand wheels rotated the gun, while the other elevated the barrel. The gun could be fired from either the left or the right hand side. Both had an identical set of controls in addition to two triggers in different places and there was a third, lanyard-firing position on the left side of the breech. The attack periscope with the small head lens has been partly raised and the commander's flagpole is visible towards the left.

U-755 (Type VIIC) showing an 88mm gun in its resting position. The wheels above the breech are part of the aiming mechanism into which speeds and ranges be can set to compensate for any differences. In the front of the bows is the 'T'-shaped head of a rotatable sound detector.

The deck guns (that is, the 88mm on Type VIIs and a 105mm forward of the conning tower plus a 37mm aft of it on Type IXs) were quick-firing guns where shells were fed singly into the breeches. The 37mm anti-aircraft gun was semi-automatic with ammunition fed in from a magazine or hopper clipped onto the top. These 37mm guns were too heavy for the smaller boats and, in addition to this, they were in such short supply that some boats were fitted with an automatic quadruple 20mm instead. The 37mm AA gun did not have a good reputation because it tended to break down or jam at critical moments and didn't have the hitting power to cope with the large, armoured aircraft that were patrolling the seas towards the end of the war.

The effectiveness of both these large anti-aircraft guns depended entirely on the efficient teamwork of the crew. One man rotated the mount while another dealt with elevation and a third and fourth fed in the shells. This required incredible coordination of hand wheels at a time when the skies had become so dangerous that the vast majority of crews never had time to practise this for long enough. Twin 37mm anti-aircraft guns, introduced towards the end of the war, produced a better

Above and opposite: An 88mm gun on display in the German U-boat Museum in Cuxhaven-Altenbruch. Although some U-boat men have claimed that ammunition for the big gun was stored in waxed cardboard tubes, this doesn't appear to be true and the majority of shells were placed inside pressure-resistant containers that were so secure that shells inside those found by divers more than fifty years after the war are still in shiny prime condition. Some shells and two such containers are standing in front of the gun.

success rate than their predecessors, but they appeared so late that only a few boats were fitted with them.

Both the single and later the twin 20mm anti-aircraft guns were easier to aim and fire. They were perfectly balanced so that they could be operated in almost the same way as a rifle with two shoulder stocks and some men achieved incredible hitting rates with them. The snag was that once the targets were within range they appeared to be moving so fast in the sights that hitting them from a pitching and rolling platform was most difficult.

The deck guns had a range of about 14,000m, meaning the shells could go much further than the lookouts could see from the top of the

Above left: Richard Thwaites holding one of the containers that used to contain 88mm ammunition.

Above right: The stunningly marked difference between 20mm and 37mm AA ammunition. The difference between the two calibres might not sound like a great deal, but the difference in size and weight was rather significant.

The 37mm gun on a Type IX had an enormous range and could reach almost as far as the 88mm, but shells had to be fed singly into the breech. The anti-aircraft gun of similar calibre used less explosive and therefore had a shorter range of less than 12,000m.

A 37mm anti-aircraft gun in the foreground with a twin 20mm to the right. The smaller guns originally came without shields, but the damage done by guns of attacking aircraft became so severe that many were provided with armoured shields. Whilst these provided some protection, they did make the aiming considerably more difficult, with gunners not always being able to see their target. The object attached to the handrails in the foreground is a navigation light with narrow slit to prevent too much light shining up into the sky.

conning tower, but hitting anything from their unstable gun platforms was extremely difficult and there was no way that the gun could be fired when an officer gave the order. Instead the aimer was told what to aim at and then he would fire the next time that spot appeared in his sights. The 20mm AA guns had a range of about 3,500–4,400m and shells from the 37mm anti-aircraft gun could travel for about the same distance, but hitting an aircraft at any range beyond a couple of kilometres was virtually impossible. Many commanders arranged the shells in such a manner that the first shots were dominated by tracer to put the pilot off his aim while he approached and then, once he was closer, the ammunition was tilted in favour of less illumination but more hitting power.

There were no hard-and-fast rules about how much ammunition should be carried and the flotilla staff in conjunction with the commander could vary quantities to suit their individual needs. Generally the quantities of ammunition carried during the first years of the war were as follows:

ATTACK U-BOATS: THEIR MAIN EXTERNAL FEATURES

Type II:	20mm	About 850 rounds
Type VII:	88mm	About 250 rounds
	20mm	About 4,380 rounds
Type IX:	105mm	Usually less than 200 rounds
	37mm	About 2,600 rounds
	20mm	About 8,500 rounds

Once aircraft had become such a major threat, ammunition was carried in many easily accessible places in considerable quantities.

A 37mm anti-aircraft gun set up in Kiel during the war for crews to become acquainted with the new weapon before trying it out for real. Many of the training guns could, of course, fire live ammunition and doubled up as part of the port's AA defences.

A quadruple 20mm anti-aircraft gun fitted to the lower gun platform of *U-870* (Type IXC/40). The reason for supplying seats for this gun and for the 37mm is to bring the weight as low down as possible to prevent some of the instability problems associated with having so much heavy gear high up. The majority of Type IX boats were later fitted with larger 37mm weapons, but these were in such short supply that the other type had to be substituted for training periods. Ammunition was fed into the gun from magazines and a rack for holding these can be seen on the side near the bottom. The additional gun platform was built immediately above the engine room or galley hatch and blocked this doorway, which had been the main entrance while in port. The raised cover in the deck planking is just visible by the ready-use ammunition containers towards the left. Since this hatch was used only in port, it did not present the gunners with an obstacle when they were at sea.

A twin 37mm anti-aircraft gun that was fitted towards the end of the war as seen on *U-534* in Birkenhead shortly after the raised boat arrived there. In Type IX boats the navigation periscope with the large head lens and the attack periscope with smaller head could both be viewed from the commander's control room inside the conning tower and thus both could be raised to the same height. In Type VII boats the sky periscope could only be used from the central control room and could thus not be raised as high as the attack periscope.

Aircraft became such a threat towards the end of the war that machine guns were fitted to the conning tower, but these did more for the morale of the crew than putting the opposition off their aim. The barrels of two machine guns are just visible and so is the head lens of the partly-raised attack periscope. The device to the right of the periscope by the man's head is a circular dipole aerial for the *Metox* radar detector that superseded the wooden 'Biscay Cross'. The men are wearing raincoats with sou'westers to cope with light rain. Each boat also carried heavier raingear to cope with storms.

ATTACK U-BOATS: THEIR MAIN EXTERNAL FEATURES

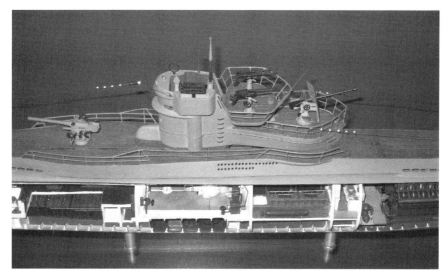

Above and below: A model on display at the International Maritime Museum in Hamburg showing how U-boat conning towers were modified to cope with the ever-increasing threat from the air. The 88mm gun was usually removed once the increased anti-aircraft armament was fitted. The device in the nearside conning tower wall is the *Hohentwiel* aerial, which had a radar detector on one side and a radar search aerial on the other. The guns are supposed to be two twin 20mm AA guns on the upper platform and a single 37mm on the lower platform – although these were generally too heavy for the Type VII and a quadruple 20mm was used instead.

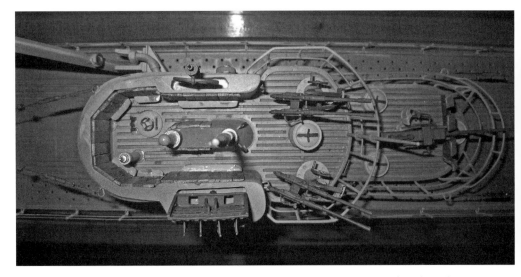

The layout of the modified conning towers, as they were fitted to larger submarines. The conning tower wall towards the top of the page has a slot for a circular radio direction finder with radio aerial attached to it. The bottom wall has a larger cavity for holding a *Hohentwiel* aerial that rotated with a radar set on one side and a radar detector on the other. In the middle are the two periscopes, the stand for the torpedo sight and the main hatch. A schnorkel fitting is just visible outside the wall towards the top. Towards the rear, on the two gun platforms are a single 37mm and two 20mm twin AA guns with the covers of the ready-use ammunition containers also visible.

Conning Towers

The strange thing about conning towers is that although the early designers at the beginning of the century made their submarines look like fish, they soon lost sight of the large dorsal fin and instead of adding this as a stabilising feature, stuck the most incredible junk onto the top or they didn't add anything at all. By the beginning of the First World War, the conning tower had already become a lookout platform, but many were flimsy structures suitable only for torturing the men that had to stand on them. This situation hadn't improved a great deal by the time the Second World War started, except that two distinctly different ideas had appeared. Britain and other nations added large conning towers with huge periscope supports rising well above the level of the men. On German boats, lookouts were always placed at the highest level with no other structures higher than their chests. It would appear that this was the limit of the designers' inventiveness and it was left to a newcomer, who was either still an apprentice or who had just

ATTACK U-BOATS: THEIR MAIN EXTERNAL FEATURES

Gustav Munzer, the architect of the Naval Memorial at Laboe near Kiel, wanted a tower so that men could climb up to see the sea as if they were looking down from a high vantage point of a ship. There were already a good number of lighthouses in the area and to stop anyone confusing the memorial with one of these, he came up with this rather dramatic shape. The memorial was officially opened on 30 May 1936, having been paid for by public subscription. Following this it became a major protagonist in the development of U-boat designs. Christoph Aschmoneit, who worked with U-boats in Kiel often climbed to the top and discovered a quirk that the top platform was often in a wind-free eddy even when a near gale was blowing over the lower platform. He took this knowledge back to work where it was used to modify U-boat conning tower designs. The monkeys' cage now at the top is a modern addition to stop parachutists from base-jumping.

U-53 (Type VIIB) from Germania Works in Kiel with the pre-war rudimentary conning tower design. This had uninterrupted, smooth edges and a slightly outward curving upper lip. The Naval Command specified that the lookouts should be at the highest point without any permanent features higher than their waists/chests. The numbers painted on the sides, the bronze eagle and the number plates on the bows were removed when the war started and many of the last mentioned were allowed to fall into the water because it was too awkward to hoist them on board. There were usually two holes in the front of the tower; one of them contained an inlet for the radio aerial and the other was a foghorn. The bulging objects on the sides, near the top of the numbers, are two horseshoe-shaped life belts and the smaller projections nearer the bottom of the numbers are navigation lights. The object above the jumping wire on the top of the conning tower is the commander's megaphone. The 88mm gun hasn't got its sights clipped in place, suggesting that maintenance work is in progress rather than artillery practice. The gun could be fired from both sides and maintaining it must have been a tedious procedure where some eighty greasing points had to be seen to. Normally when not in use the gun would be fitted with watertight tampions at both ends.

ATTACK U-BOATS: THEIR MAIN EXTERNAL FEATURES

risen from that level, to improve this. Christoph Aschmoneit, who worked in the dockyards in Kiel, frequently visited the naval memorial at Laboe, not so much to pay homage to the men lost during the war, but to enjoy the magnificent views from the top of the huge tower. There he became aware of the quirk that the upper platform was often in a wind-free eddy even

U-47 (Type VIIB) which torpedoed HMS *Royal Oak* in the Royal Navy's anchorage at Scapa Flow in October 1939. The emblem of the snorting bull was not added until after this raid and can therefore be used to help date this picture as having been taken after that time. Note that some elementary modification has been made to the conning tower to provide a deflector half way up. The torpedo loading gear can be seen assembled at the rear near the open galley hatch. In front of it is the dismantled mount for a 20mm anti-aircraft gun. The bulge at the base of the conning tower, housing the magnetic compass, also contains an emergency life-saving connections marked with a cross inside a square. This mark was welded proud of the wall so that a diver could find it when murky water might make it difficult to see. The square marked an emergency compressed air inlet for blowing the diving tanks and there was also a circle with a cross to mark an inlet for ventilating the accommodation areas. Men carrying heavy ammunition for the 88mm gun from the magazine below the radio room had to clamber down the back of the conning tower and then negotiate this narrow deck with the heavy shells.

when a gale raged on the slightly lower level. Taking this concept back to work, he eventually managed to influence his superiors to make use of this feature to improve the conning towers of U-boats.

The generic development of conning towers is not terribly difficult to follow, despite there having been vast variations of the basic theme. Initially, that is before the war and up to the end of 1940, the general consensus of opinion was that aircraft couldn't harm submarines because they would dive long before anything in the air could get close enough to attack. This leaves one with the question, why then did the Navy add an anti-aircraft gun? Bearing in mind that the German battleship and cruisers of the Channel Dash of 1942 were attacked by canvas-covered Swordfish aircraft, it is quite likely that the designers might have thought the single 20mm anti-aircraft gun was adequate defence against such cumbersome flying machines. Whatever thought process may have given rise to placing this weapon to the rear of the conning tower, it was as early as 1941 that the Germans discovered that it was not of much use there.

During the first months of the war it was even too small for putting a shot across the bows, the traditional way of stopping a ship. Some commanders used the gun for blowing out the windows of the bridge when a ship refused to stop or when there was no-one on the bridge to take any notice of the approaching submarine's visual signals. There were only a few gun battles with aircraft until these started to hit back with a vengeance from 1941 onwards. One of the first battles against aircraft took place during the first few days of the war when *U-30* (Kapitänleutnant Fritz-Julius Lemp) saved the lives of some attacking airmen, although they hadn't been shot at. Fragments from their own exploding bombs had brought them down.

The big problem was that any effort to hit a fast-moving aircraft was likely to be frustrated by the rolling and pitching of the gun platform and to make this even worse, the British mounted relatively small sheets of armour in front of the main components such as engines, instruments and the crew. Once the aircraft was sideways-on to the U-boat, it was almost impossible to hit because it was so close and moving too fast.

To overcome this, Germany responded by increasing the anti-aircraft armament and in doing so produced a wide range of variations, but all followed the same basic principle. The existing gun platform was enlarged to hold two twin 20mm and a lower platform was added with either a 37mm semi-automatic or a quadruple 20mm. Whilst this combination had some initial successes during several highly dramatic duels with aircraft, the hitting power wasn't sufficient to combat the majority of air attacks.

ATTACK U-BOATS: THEIR MAIN EXTERNAL FEATURES

U-34 (Type VIIA) built at Germania Works in Kiel. The commander (Kapitänleutnant Ernst Sobe) commissioning the boat gives a good indication of size and shows how difficult it must have been to bring ammunition down the ladders for the guns. This photograph was taken on 12 September 1936, at a time when it had not yet been decided to fit an anti-aircraft gun to the rear of the conning tower. Instead there was a 20mm mounted on the upper deck to the rear of the tower. The vents under the commander's feet allow air to pass to the main ventilation ducts. The large horseshoe by the '3' is a life ring.

An early Type IX at Deschimag AG Weser with the modified type of gun platform already installed. The 20mm anti-aircraft gun could be separated from its mount and a horseshoe-shaped life ring has been left lying on the deck. In the middle are two periscope supports surrounded by some casing and a sighting compass is attached to the rear edge (nearest the camera). Periscope openings were often covered with lids to prevent tools and rubbish from falling into the shafts and perhaps damaging the extra-smooth edges that allow the periscope to slide easily. The commander's flagpole (to the left of the man sitting on the railings in the background) and the main flagpole at the rear of gun platform were usually taken below when the boat dived. On the forward edge of the conning tower wall, towards the left, one can make out a slot for housing the circular radio direction finder and the hole towards its left holds an extendible radio aerial that could be raised as high as the periscopes.

This has been identified as *U-32* (Type VIIA) and the hatbands with *U-bootsflottille Saltzwedel* suggests that this photograph was taken between April 1937 and the beginning of the war. Notice that the men on the bridge are protected by a sheet of canvas, the same method that was found to have been highly inadequate during the First World War, so one wonders why this was adopted again many years later. This shows that the boats of the Second World War were not as advanced as some people have made out. In the foreground is a mount for a 20mm anti-aircraft gun but without the gun screwed in position. The red-and-white-striped rescue buoy with light can be seen in its fitting on the deck. A compass with sighting device in position can just be made out between the two men on the bridge. The men on the right (front), wearing black leathers without large lapels, are mechanics taking a breather while off duty. Note the spelling of the flotilla's name. Salt in German is *Salz* but the flotilla was named after Oberleutnant zur See Reinhold Saltzwedel, a commander who gained the Pour le Mérite before he was killed during the First World War.

U-30 (Type VIIA) with a further modification to the conning tower. The radio operator, George Högel, painted the emblem of the dog after the beginning of the war, when the deflector half way up the conning tower had been added as a substantial feature. The all-important air ducts leading down from the top of the conning tower terminated at deck level during earlier days and it looks as if an extension to raise them higher has been added on to the outside of the wall as an afterthought. The navigation light is visible and note that the 20mm anti-aircraft gun has been moved onto an enlarged platform to the rear of the conning rather than sitting lower down on the upper deck.

At one stage some boats were converted into aircraft traps with an additional gun platform forward of the conning tower. The reason for fitting this was to provide the boat with a better chance when attacked from the front because by this time RAF Coastal Command had established that U-boat anti-aircraft guns could only fire astern and was taking steps to avoid that zone. But in practice these platforms turned out to be little more than bloody death traps for the gunners and the additional weight so high up caused such stability problems that some experts were convinced this heavy armament was directly responsible for the disappearance of some U-boats. The problem with the aircraft-trap conversions is that the documentation of these appears to be incomplete and leaves a few unresolved mysteries. It is well known that they were employed fairly unsuccessfully in the Bay of Biscay, but there is also some evidence that they were used in Norway and at least one boat, *U-673*, probably operated in the Arctic in such a configuration.

ATTACK U-BOATS: THEIR MAIN EXTERNAL FEATURES

It looks likely that this Type IXC/40 is *U-889* and that this picture was taken after it had surrendered at the end of the war. There is a lot of junk lying around that would not normally be seen on an operational conning tower. The wooden lining along the walls was added towards the end of the war to make the bridge more comfortable for lookouts and notice also that struts were put on top of the deck slats to make them less slippery. In the far background is a 37mm anti-aircraft gun on the lower platform and two twin 20mm are nearer the camera. The torpedo sight, of which a variety of different models were installed on U-boats, can be seen in the foreground on the right. The special binoculars that fitted on top did not have any sighting grid inside them and produced the same type of view that the men saw through ordinary glasses. They differed in being water and pressure resistant so that (theoretically) they would not be damaged if they were left in position during an alarm dive. The two supports in the middle contain the sky or navigation periscope with the large head lens nearest the camera and the slightly raised attack periscope further away. Between them is a tall stalk with the round dipole aerial of the *Metox* radar detector. There seems to be a round bit of something resting on top of this aerial. The grating in the bulge of the conning tower wall towards the left is the top of the air duct leading down to the engine room and the rectangular box to the right houses the rotatable *Hohentwiel* aerial with a radar detector on one side and a radar search aerial on the other.

A Type VIIC showing the general appearance of conning towers after the start of the war, with the upper wind deflector inverted from how it was during earlier times and with the spray deflector half way up the tower forming a dominant feature. The insulators in the jumping wires are clearly visible and note that the gun sight has been clipped into position. The bracket below it, just above the hand wheels, could be turned outwards to help hold the gunner in place so that he could use both hands for turning the wheel. The aerial intake and the foghorn are both visible.

Early conning towers were fitted with two periscopes, the tops of the ventilation shafts, a torpedo sight and the main hatch. Everything else appeared to have come as an afterthought, to be squeezed in wherever there was room. What is not so obvious in photographs is that the walls were also modified to provide better protection from splinters. Many were armoured and some were even provided with a cupboard-like box that was supposed to serve as a shelter, but no one found that this worked very well. The shells being fired from the aircraft caused relatively little direct damage and most injuries were caused when they started bouncing from one armoured wall to another.

Hatches

The torpedo hatches were built at an angle to allow for easy loading, but otherwise were the same size and shape as all the other hatches. The hatches below the upper deck usually had a grating or cover over them so that men would not fall into the gap between the upper deck and the pressure hull.

Hatches going straight down were fitted between two supporting frames, but the oblique nature of the torpedo mechanism meant these loading hatches had to cut through several of the all-important frames, leaving a considerable weak section in the design. After capturing *U-570*, a Royal Navy officer wrote that he was surprised to find the Germans had solved this problem by bolting special supports into the missing sections to strengthen this weak link. These thick supporting struts are visible here below the bow torpedo-loading hatch of *U-995*.

ATTACK U-BOATS: THEIR MAIN EXTERNAL FEATURES

Right: The U-boat's front door – the conning tower hatch, showing how narrow the opening was for men to squeeze through. The overweight people seen walking around these days would never fit through.

Below: Looking down from the main conning tower hatch of *U-995* in Laboe. All operational U-boats had another water and pressure-resistant hatch between the conning tower compartment and the central control room.

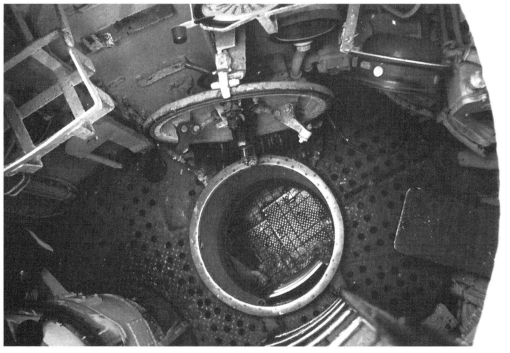

Kapitänleutnant Reinhard Hardegen, as seen from below, illustrating the tightness of the hatches.

ATTACK U-BOATS: THEIR MAIN EXTERNAL FEATURES

Radar

Germany had some working radar equipment a few years before Britain and was using it successfully as early as 1938. The problem was that the radar signals travelled considerably further than the distance from which an echo could be obtained. This meant that any radio operator capable of picking up radar impulses could locate the ship that was sending out the radar transmission without the sender knowing that he had been located. This was a definite drawback for the weak German Navy because the ability to hide from superior forces was considered to be one of its strongest assets. As a result German radar was developed as a rangefinder for training guns after the target had been visually sighted and radar then made it possible to continue shooting when interrupted by fog or smoke. The German equipment was so good that the gunnery training cruiser *Königsberg* could get in and out of any port in the worst visibility because the radar on board made it possible

On the left is a radio direction finder that consisted of two semicircular sections that were joined at the top and bottom. The whole contraption could be rotated from the radio room to give some indication as to where radio signals were coming from. These rings were used for homing in on other U-boats at sea, especially during periods of poor visibility when it was impossible to take bearings on the sun or stars. The wooden 'Biscay Cross' that served as aerial for the *Metox* radar detector had a variety of slightly different designs, but all of them had to be taken below when the boat dived and therefore they had to fit through the hatches.

The circular dipole aerial for the *Metox* radar detector that replaced the wooden 'Biscay Cross' with the original censor's stamp still in visible.

Hard times in the Bay of Biscay with a wooden cross-like radar detection aerial for the *Metox* receiver in position. Wooden slats have been added to the conning tower walls and the extendible radio aerial on the left is partly raised. The grids in both ends of the wall are the tops of air ducts with the main supply going to the engine room.

to 'see' the buoys marking both sides of the deep-water channel. The big drawback came at the start of the war, when Hitler ordered all research that could not be completed within a year or so to be abandoned.

British radar made its first significant contribution during March 1940 when *U-99* and *U-100*, with the aces Kapitänleutnant Otto Kretschmer and Kapitänleutnant Joachim Schepke, were sunk. Following that, radar continued to play a major role in the Battles of the Atlantic, without the Germans at first being aware that it was being used. One reason for this was that radar lost sight of the target once the time between sending out the signal and receiving the echo became too short, and this happened around the same time as the escort appeared on the U-boat's horizon, where it was spotted by lookouts on the conning tower. The escort then continued running blind, often passing close to the surfaced U-boat without spotting its low silhouette in the darkness.

The crunch with radar came during the winter of 1941/42 when Germany realised it was being used to locate U-boats which gave rise to a variety of countermeasures being introduced. At the same time the old German radar experts were recalled to help find ways of using it for finding convoys on the high seas.

Whilst the development of radar is beyond the scope of this book, the aerials fitted to the top of conning towers play a significant role when identifying old photographs. The first radar-detecting aerial, the so-called 'Biscay Cross' connected to what was called *Metox* (after its French manufacturer), consisted of a rough wooden cross with wires strung around the outside and had a lead running down through the open hatch to the radio room. The aerial had to be turned by hand and taken down when the boat dived. This equipment was in such short supply that there were several cases of boats passing out of the dangerous Bay of Biscay handing the receiver and aerial over to an inbound U-boat. The aerial was quickly improved and a circular dipole version appeared that did not need to be dismantled when diving. The range over which radar signals could be picked up increased as well and in 1942 there was a stage where both the old and the new versions were being used. The new one warned the U-boat that an aircraft with radar was in the vicinity and the old equipment indicated that it was close enough to attack and therefore triggered the diving process. Following this initial stage, a variety of other aerials appeared to play a significant role in the war at sea.

The word radar was already reasonably well known in Germany, but used most often in horror stories rather than scientific accounts and the navy distinguished between two different pieces of equipment.

Above: U-172 (Type IXC). The peculiar box on the front of the conning tower is a later type of aerial for a radar detection device, of which a variety of different types were tried out. On the top of the tower, between the two men, one can see a side-on view of the circular radio direction finder.

Opposite: These hedgehog-like aerials around the front of the conning tower were an attempt to provide U-boats with a radio search device to help find convoys. The device was originally called a *Dezimeter-telefonie-gerät*, which was abbreviated to *DeTe Gerät* (DeTe Apparatus). The majority of the crew would not have been aware of its function and called it *Dre~turm~gerät* (Revolving Turret Apparatus) because the early devices that were fitted to surface ships rotated. When this radar equipment was later modified for use in U-boats, it was at first fixed to the conning tower as shown here, meaning it was necessary for the boat to turn in a circle to complete an all-round sweep. The aerials were later added to a rotating device on the top of the conning tower. The stamp on top of this photo is an original censor's mark saying the photo is restricted and may not be published. Note the circular radar detection aerial under the smudge by the man on the top. And also note that the single jumping wire running down to the bows has been replaced by a double set to provide a gap for the radar signals to pass through without interference. The bracket for supporting the gunner has been turned outwards to be ready for use.

Above left and right: This wartime photograph shows part of the circular radar detection device on the left. Note that the circular radio direction finder on the right has another radio aerial attached to it. The device that the man is rotating by hand is quite rare and contains two different radar detection aerials on opposite sides. It was fitted inside the circular radio direction finder on some operational boats.

The problems for Germany came shortly after the discovery that radar was being used against U-boats when experts realised the Allies had a variety of different short-wave radar sets. This is significant inasmuch that the early German radar pioneers who developed the DeTe Apparatus thought that only long-wave radar would work and short-wave radio ranging would be impossible. So this discovery during the middle of the war came as a major shock to the Germans. On the right is a close-up of the short-wave *Tunis* radar detection aerial with the 9cm aerial for the *Naxos* receiver on the left and the 3cm for the *Mücke* or *Fliege* ('Gnat' or 'Fly') on the right. Tested originally aboard *U-889* (Type IXC/40), this device became operational towards the end of the war and in some cases was added to fit inside the circular ring of the radio direction finder. *Naxos* was a name given to a short-wave radar receiver that came into service during the summer of 1943. This extremely rare device was photographed at the *U-534* Museum at the Woodside Ferry Terminal (opposite Liverpool) on the Mersey.

Towards the end of the war a number of devices were fitted to the tops of conning towers for detecting Allied radar and some also had radar search facilities, but none of them played a significant role in the war at sea. This is one field where the German education system backfired on the navy's officer corps. Candidates had pass university entrance examinations at school to be accepted as officer cadets and many of them came without a great deal of technical knowledge, having concentrated more on Latin than technology. As result a good number were blissfully ignorant of the technology that was provided to help them.

FuMB and FuMO meaning *Funk~mess~beobachtung* (meaning a device for detecting radar impulses) and *Funk~mess~ortung* (meaning radio location – radar), respectively. The other words that crept into this sphere were *Funk~mess~gerät* (radio ranging apparatus), *Funk~peil~gerät* (radio direction finder) and *Funk~mess~erkennung* (radar recognition). Only a few books have appeared dealing with this highly technical subject of radar, but it is possible to find some excellent Internet pages on the subject.

The need to counter the underwater sound detection device, known as Asdic during the Second World War and now called Sonar, also left a visible mark on the outside of U-boats, but photos of this are exceedingly rare and even when found, it is not easy to spot. Known under the cover name of *Alberich*, it consisted of 5mm thick rubber sheeting that was capable of seriously reducing the echo obtained by sonar. This idea, tried out as early as 1941 when it was applied experimentally to *U-67* (Type IXC), produced good results but failed miserably once used operationally. The big problem was that the sheeting had to be applied in a dry location, away from rain and dust and even when attached to the hull under ideal conditions, the sheets peeled off to start producing their own weird flapping noise. This sounded so unlike anything else that was heard at sea, that it became an obvious giveaway for listeners and even the dimmest Asdic operators were likely to notice it. Yet several U-boats that were coated with this absorbent skin reported a significant reduction in escorts detecting the presence of the U-boat. So, it seems to have worked well, if only a method could have been found to attach it firmly to steel.

Schnorkels

Schnorkels, air supply pipes for running diesel engines while submerged, were first used before the war by the Dutch Navy to prevent their Far Eastern boats from having to surface into the hot sun. They were introduced by Commander J.J. Wichers and appeared to have worked reasonably well, but they were abandoned again when the Germans captured some boats during their 1940 invasion of the Netherlands. The Kriegsmarine couldn't see a reason for developing such gear. The idea was picked up again towards the end of 1942 when U-boats founds themselves being hit hard by attacking aircraft.

The first German schnorkel was tried out aboard *U-58* during the summer of 1943. Following that, the first operational system was installed in September of that year aboard *U-236*, but by the time

U-889 (Type IXC/40) shortly after the war with its schnorkel in the extended position. The circular radio direction finder that is housed in the conning tower wall is also extended and this has a radio aerial attached to it. Also visible within the ring is the head of the partly extended attack periscope and there is also a removable flagpole.

U-889 with the schnorkel sitting inside its storage box between the upper deck and the pressure hull. Nearest the camera is a circular dipole aerial for a radar detector and behind that one can see the rubber-covered structure of the head valve. Beyond that is the exhaust pipe and the bulge nearest the conning tower is where the schnorkel butts onto the conning tower's air duct.

of the D-Day invasion in June 1944 there were still many U-boats in dangerous waters without this lifesaving aid. Schnorkels did not get the failing U-boats back onto the offensive, but gave them an opportunity of escaping from the ferociousness of the Allied attacks by providing a slight advantage, making it possible to escape rather than to be sunk.

A considerable variety of different designs were tried out and can still be seen in old photographs. Despite this variation, they all functioned on two basic principles. The new Type XXI and XXIII electro-boats were fitted with versions that could be raised in a similar manner to periscopes, but there wasn't enough room in the older boats to accommodate such space-consuming ducts. Therefore schnorkels were hinged below the outside deck near the front of the conning tower. When not in use they fitted into the space under the outside deck and when raised they clipped into a bracket at the top of the conning tower, which supported the cumbersome duct. There was a large valve at the top to prevent too much seawater from entering during turbulent seas and just below this was an exhaust pipe for hopefully dispersing diesel fumes in the water, rather than squelching them up into the air. In addition to a wide variety of different head valves, each system had a well at its deepest point for collecting water that might wash through the top opening so that it could be pumped out again with existing pumps.

Although highly precarious and often most uncomfortable for the crew, these systems did provide the difference between meagre existence and a quick death by making it possible for the submerged U-boat to cruise at a maximum of about 5kt. For much of the time progress was much slower and the device was used more to charge the batteries than to make progress under water. By the time schnorkels were introduced it was possible for Allied radar to pick up the head of an extended attack periscope at a range of about 2000 yards (1.8km), so it was necessary to fit each schnorkel head valve with some type of radar-absorbing material and with a radar-detecting aerial. Despite this, it was still possible to spot schnorkel heads during daylight and aircrews were especially trained to keep an eye open for the tell-tale signs of them being used.

Torpedoes

During the Second World War Germany had two different types of torpedoes that could be discharged from U-boats. Their designation of G7 was a throwback to earlier years when they were known under the

ATTACK U-BOATS: THEIR MAIN EXTERNAL FEATURES

A G7a torpedo being loaded. Type II boats were so small that torpedoes had to be loaded backwards from the bows before they could be pushed forwards into the tubes. Type IXs were large enough for the loading process to proceed without too much ado, but on Type VIIs, as seen here, the deck was too short with not enough space between the torpedo hatch and the 88mm gun so the gun had to be turned sideways for the loading process to work. The lowering mechanism was manual, with a man having to rotate a handle when lowering the torpedo into the boat. This device can be seen at the edge of the picture by the man on the right.

code name *Gerade~lauf~apperat* (running in a straight line apparatus). The '7' referred to the length (c. 7m) and distinguished it from a smaller variety that was later developed for use by aircraft and small torpedo boats. Surface raiders used other, older varieties and towards the end of the war Germany developed faster versions, but these did not see operational service.

The first, G7a, was powered by an internal combustion engine, which was injected with compressed air and steam so that it could run underwater. The other variety, G7e, had batteries and an electric motor.

These had a considerably shorter range and slower speed than the other type. Their performance was roughly as follows:

	G7a	G7e
Length:	7.2m	7.2m
Diameter:	53.34cm	53.45cm
Weight:	1.530t	1.600t
Warhead:	300kg	300kg
Range/speed:	6km @ 44kt	5km @ 30kt
	8km @ 40kt	
	12km @ 30kt	

Despite its better performance, the great disadvantage of the G7a was that it left a noticeable trail of oil and bubbles, making it possible to spot it as it approached its target.

Up to the beginning of the war it was still necessary to aim the entire submarine at the target, but angle deflectors were already in existence and the majority of boats could aim torpedoes without too much regard to their position. The final adjustments, made while the torpedoes were in their tubes ready to be discharged, were dialled into a torpedo calculator and transmitted to an indicator by the torpedo tubes. A pointer showed the desired settings and all the mechanics had to do was to adjust their hand wheels so that a second set of indicators pointed to the same position. Once the two matched, the settings in the torpedo were correct. Statements in some books that the optical sights on the top of the conning tower automatically made the torpedo adjustments are not true. Early on during the war there were several incidents where the pressing of the firing trigger in the conning tower failed to fire the torpedoes, so the order was transmitted verbally through the boat so that the torpedo mechanics would also press the trigger that was attached to each tube.

Early torpedoes travelled in a straight line until they ran out of power, when theoretically they should have dropped to the bottom of the sea, but there many cases of faulty torpedoes passing under their target and then exploding at the end of their run. Torpedoes could be adjusted to detonate in one of two ways. Either they were set to run under the target and were then magnetically detonated to break a merchant ship in two or they were set run nearer the surface to be triggered by an impact detonator.

A training torpedo with a red-and-white striped head that incorporated a lamp so that it was possible to follow its course at night.

The torpedo crisis that dominated the beginning of the war was exceedingly complex because it involved more than one fault, which was not recognised at the time.

This basic principle of running in a straight line was improved towards the end of 1942 when an anti-convoy torpedo, called 'Curly' by the Allied navies, was added to the armoury. In Germany it was known as FAT from *Feder~apperat~torpedo* (spring apparatus torpedo), but many men were unaware of its proper name and called it *Flächen~absuchenden~torpedo* (surface searching torpedo). This was later further developed into the LUT, from *Lagen~unabhängigen~torpedo* (independent bearing torpedo), which could be discharged from depths of up to about 50m. The aiming and firing process had hardly been changed and these new torpedoes ran in straight lines towards their targets, but then, if they missed, they would start running in a loop, to perhaps hit another ship in the convoy. The length of the straight run was variable and could be adjusted shortly before firing.

The big problem that remained for the German Navy was that from 1941 onwards U-boats found themselves in positions where escorts came bearing down on them at high speed. Avoiding this sort of attack was easy at first because the escort had detected its target by radar and lost contact roughly the same time as U-boat lookouts spotted the attacker. So, at night it was a simple case of merely moving out of the

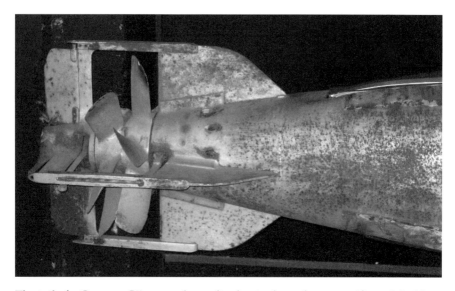

The tail of a German G7a torpedo on display in the rather magnificent Maritime Museum in Zeebrugge (Belgium) where they also have an incredible post-war Russian submarine.

The tail of a G7e torpedo on display at the International Maritime Museum in Hamburg (Germany). In this case a midget submarine is carrying the torpedo, which often had some of the batteries removed because the weight of an ordinary torpedo was too heavy for such small craft.

ATTACK U-BOATS: THEIR MAIN EXTERNAL FEATURES

A G7a torpedo being lowered into a Type IX U-boat. In the foreground is the 105mm gun.

A G7a torpedo being lowered into a Type IX U-boat. The winding mechanism for stopping the torpedo from falling out of control is just out of the picture, towards the right. The gear towards the left is for pulling the torpedo out of its storage tube that is located below the upper (outside) deck.

way and with the radar too close to get an echo, the unique advantage had been lost. This situation didn't last long. It was a simple matter of leaving the ship with the radar set where she was and directing another escort towards the U-boat.

This problem of small warships approaching head-on at high speed had been foreseen in Germany, where the development of the necessary countermeasure was already in production. It took the form of an acoustic torpedo that homed in on any significant noise in the vicinity and, at the same time, it had also had the ability to distinguish between a ship and a towed noise-making decoy. Known as the *Zaun~könig* (Wren) or T5, this torpedo first saw service during the autumn of 1943. Unknown to the German Navy, it had an intrinsic fault that caused it to detonate behind the target. Some torpedoes got close enough to blow off propellers, but the majority exploded far enough away not to seriously damage the ship. The U-boat had to dive deep at that critical moment of firing to prevent the acoustic torpedo from homing in on the boat that had fired it. The men in the submerged U-boat heard the detonation but were often unaware that this hadn't sunk their target. The acoustic torpedo had a success rate of not much more than 10 per cent.

Torpedo Mines

Small but quite sophisticated torpedo mines and air mines for dropping from aircraft were developed after the end of the First World War and by 1939 the TMA (Torpedo Mine Type A) was already being replaced by an improved Type B. This, in turn, was enlarged to produce a third type that was identified by the letter 'C'. Three TMBs or two TMCs could be accommodated in one torpedo tube to make them an important weapon during the first winter of the war when Germany was faced by an embarrassing shortage of torpedoes. While the small Type II boats could carry only five torpedoes, they did have room for up to eighteen mines, which were used for a significant number of attacks against British harbours on east, west and south coasts. Much of this interesting offensive has hardly been documented. Torpedo tubes required a special modification to eject these mines and both commanders and torpedo mechanics also needed additional training to use them. The dedicated Types XB and VIID

Photos of torpedo mines are exceedingly rare. There were three main types; either three or two of them fitted into the same space as one torpedo.

minelayers used a larger shaft mine that did not fit into torpedo tubes. The statistics for torpedo mines were as follows:

	TMA	TMB	TMC
Length:	2.31m	2.31m	3.39m
Weight:	800kg	740kg	1,115kg
Explosive charge:	215kg	580kg	935kg

The following boats were definitely fitted with the minelaying modification and used as minelayers during the first nine months of the war, although a few were recalled before being able to carry out their operation and several undertook more than one minelaying operation: *U-13, U-15, U-16, U-17, U-19, U-20, U-21, U-22, U-23, U-24, U-28, U-29, U-30, U-31, U-32, U-33, U-34, U-48, U-53, U-58, U-59, U-60* and *U-61*.

Rockets

Rockets launched from below the surface were probably used operationally in the Black Sea and there is possible evidence of at least two U-boats carrying rockets to the United States. This cropped up unexpectedly during the early 1980s while I was digging through recently released files in the Royal Navy's Submarine Museum in Gosport. Among the papers were two separate reports from escort commanders about their attacks on submerged submarines. Depth charges dropped in both cases resulted in what was described as a large underwater fire lasting for several minutes. Both the submarine expert 'Professor' Gus Britton and the Director of the Museum, Commander Richard Compton-Hall, said that the accounts must have been written by over-enthusiastic and inexperienced escort commanders, who imagined the fire. Sadly, as a result of their comments, I didn't record the details and put the papers back into the huge pile where they had come from. Both boats were in the Atlantic, probably heading for the United States and even now I sometimes wonder whether they were carrying some type of underwater rocket system for use against the large cities there.

The rockets in the Black Sea are better documented and it seems likely that they were used by the small Type IIB boats against Russian oil depots along its eastern shore. Gerd Enders first uncovered this story, after he had written his magnificent book about the Black Sea U-boats. Searching through logbooks after they had been released he was surprised to come across a couple of comments saying the 'throwers' were a great success. Not knowing what this meant he approached the men who were in command in the area during the war but no one could throw any light on the subject until he traced the men who manned the U-boats involved. From them he discovered the incredible tale.

It would appear that Type IIB boats were too small to carry anything much bigger than a 20mm AA gun and their only effective weapon was the torpedoes they carried. Yet these were useless against the huge oil installations along the Russian Black Sea coast and therefore the rockets were fitted and used. Their targets covered a large enough area that any hit within them was likely to cause a significant fire.

Photos showing rocket trials with *U-511* (Kapitänleutnant Friedrich Steinhoff) in May–June 1942, where the launching racks are attached to the upper deck of the submarine, have become quite famous. One of the major problems was that this cumbersome apparatus made it difficult to handle the boat and there were severe steering problems with the rockets the moment they passed from water to air. The rockets used in the Black Sea were basically the same as those seen in the photos of *U-511*, but the bottoms of the launching racks were attached to the boat's keel while the upper ends fastened onto the pressure hull. The difficulty with aiming was not a problem given the large size of the intended targets.

A solid-fuel rocket photographed during trials aboard *U-511* under Kapitänleutnant Friedrich Steinhoff. Similar rockets were later used successfully against Russian targets along the shores of the Black Sea. On *U-511* they were attached to the upper deck, but the bottoms of the operational ones were attached to the keel, to slope upwards at an angle so that the tops of the firing tubes were fixed below the waterline of a surfaced submarine. This was so well concealed that even the crew was at first not aware that it had been fitted in their absence.

Chapter 8

Internal Features of a Type VIIC

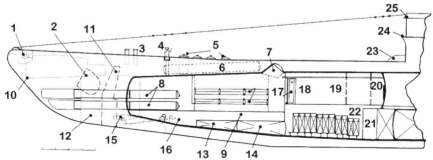

Bows
1. Hook for attaching towing hawser.
2. Anchor on starboard (right-hand) side.
3. Bollards for attaching mooring ropes. (Another set on the bows is not shown.)
4. Detachable capstan head powered by the anchor chain motor.
5. Water and pressure-resistant containers for inflatable life rafts. There were similar hatches near the guns for holding ready-use ammunition.

INTERNAL FEATURES OF A TYPE VIIC

6. Storage tube for spare torpedo. Type VIIs had one in the bows and another one near the stern. Type IXs were large enough to have these arranged in pairs.
7. Torpedo loading hatch.
8. Torpedo tubes.
9. Space for four reload torpedoes below the deck and another two above the deck.
10. Stabilising tank.
11. Anchor chain locker.
12. Position of diving tank.
13. Trim tank.
14. Torpedo compensating tank.
15. Hydroplanes.
16. Manual hydroplane controls with gauges for emergencies.
17. The heads (lavatory) on the port side with sound-retarding bulkhead separating it from the bow compartment.
18. Warrant officers' accommodation except for the torpedo mechanic who had a bunk in the bow compartment.
19. Commissioned officers' accommodation.

20. Commander's 'cabin' on the port side and radio room with underwater listening room opposite on the starboard side.
21. Magazine for gun ammunition.
22. Battery compartment.
23. Magnetic compass.
24. Wave and spray deflector.
25. Wind deflector.

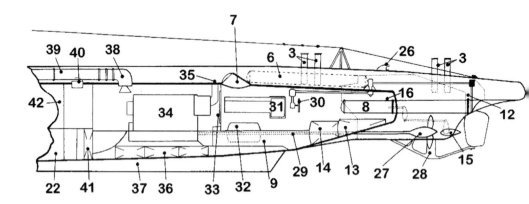

Stern
3. Bollards for mooring.
6. Torpedo storage tube.
7. Torpedo loading hatch.
8. Torpedo tube.
9. Storage for one torpedo between the electric motors.
10. Stabilising tank in the stern not shown in diagram.
12. Position of diving tank.
13. Trim tank.
14. Torpedo compensation tank.
15. Hydroplane.
16. Manual hydroplane controls with gauges for emergencies.
22. Battery compartment.
26. Rear light.
27. Propellers.
28. Propeller guard and rudder bracket.
29. Propeller shaft (clutches not shown).
30. Emergency steering wheel.
31. Electric motor controls.
32. Electric motors.
33. Sound-retarding bulkhead.

INTERNAL FEATURES OF A TYPE VIIC

34. Diesel engine.
35. Exhaust pipe leading to exterior.
36. Oil tanks. There was a ready-use fuel tank under the ceiling above the diesel engines, which was filled daily.
37. Hollow box keel for holding ballast.
38. Fresh air intake for diesel engines.
39. Fresh air duct.
40. Galley hatch with galley on port side and a spare head in the starboard side.
41. A variety of water tanks for the galley.
42. Petty officers' accommodation with stern battery compartment underneath.

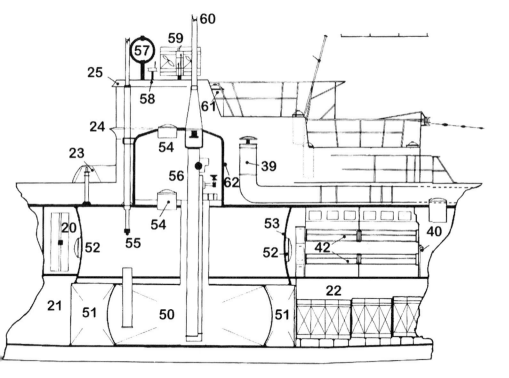

The Central Control Room
20. Commander's accommodation on the port side and radio room with underwater sound detector on the opposite side.
21. Magazine for gun ammunition.
22. Battery compartment under petty officers' accommodation.
23. Magnetic compass that could be viewed by the helmsman through an illuminated periscope.

24. Wave or spray deflector.
25. Wind deflector.
39. Main air intake with duct leading to the engine room. Many had the intake extended to reach up to the top of the conning tower.
40. Galley with hatch, which served as main entry and exit point while in port.
42. Petty officers' accommodation.
50. Main diving tanks with periscope and rod aerial wells.
51. Oil tank.
52. Hatch through water and pressure-tight bulkhead.
53. Curved pressure-resistant bulkheads on both ends of the central control room.
54. Hatch.
55. Sky or navigation periscope eyepieces. (Type IX conning towers were large enough for this periscope to be viewed from the conning tower room as well.)
56. Commander's control room for submerged attacks, with torpedo calculator (not shown).
57. Radio direction finder aerial.
58. Circular dipole aerial that replaced the wooden 'Biscay Cross' for the radar detector.
59. Rotating *Hohentwiel* aerial with radar on one side and radar detector on the other.
60. Attack periscope with small head and saddle viewed from the conning tower room.
61. Ready-use ammunition containers.
62. Extension of the pressure hull.

Chapter 9

The Crew: Key U-boat Positions

Electro and Diesel Mechanics

Each boat had a man of warrant officer rank as motor mechanic and another with similar rank as diesel mechanic, supported by senior petty officers with a number of ratings to help them. Both the motor and the diesel mechanics stood six-hour watches and senior petty officers were in charge of the controls when their bosses were off duty.

The noise of the diesel engines was so loud that it was impossible to hold a conversation near them while they were running. The scene in the film *Das Boot*, where the commander chatted with the diesel mechanic would have been impossible in reality. Even the alarm bells that were capable of waking the dead could not be heard and engine room lights started flashing when alarm or telegraph bells rang.

Das Boot also shows the diesel mechanic opening taps on the side of the engine, allowing flames to shoot out. Several people have asked how this was possible when smoking was not allowed inside the submarine. The reason for allowing the dramatic flames to shoot out was to test whether each cylinder was firing correctly and the men were not allowed to smoke inside the boat because the batteries underneath the accommodation compartments gave off an explosive mixture of hydrogen and oxygen when charging and discharging. In U-boats this was vented into the living spaces. There were no batteries under the engines and this area was well ventilated with its own direct air supply, meaning there was little danger of explosive gasses collecting there. On several occasions where men accidentally triggered an explosion in the battery compartments, mostly during training, they were seriously injured. (Such disasters were easily triggered by sparks from torches or from unprotected light bulbs.)

Heinrich Brink, *Elektro~ober~maschinist* of *U-98*. Keeping a written record of all changes to the system was part of the daily routine and a small desk was provided for the purpose.

THE CREW: KEY U-BOAT POSITIONS

A mock-up of the electric control panel in a training establishment.

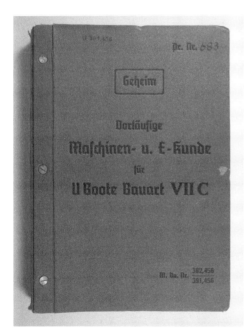

Above left and right: Every aspect of U-boat life was controlled by official handbooks and it is amazing that so many with a multitude of shapes and sizes were taken to sea.

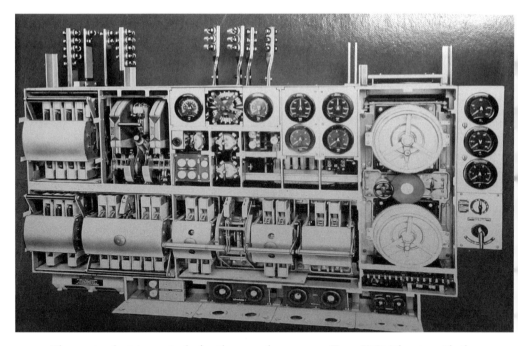

The main electric controls for the very long-range Type IXD-2 boats with the front panel having been taken off, as shown in the official handbook. Speed was controlled by levers rather than hand wheels. This board controlled the motors as well as other electrical gear and could even adjust the electricity that was allowed to flow into the galley's cookers.

Both the diesel and motor rooms contained far more machinery than one finds under the bonnet of a car and although this ran on its own without having to make adjustments for much of the time, there was a long list of maintenance checks that had to be carried out continuously. Oiling moving parts was an essential part of running this old machinery. Engines that ran completely without supervision did not appear until the end of the Second World War, when the new Type XXIs and XXIII were brought into service. In addition to maintenance, there were other machines that needed constant attention. Perhaps the most troublesome of these were the air compressors which made so much noise that a modern business would not be allowed to run them in a large hall without thick ear protection for the operators. It is impossible to imagine how men cooped up in a small submarine coped with such dreadful noise.

Spare parts for machinery that was likely to wear out were supplied and often packed in wooden boxes with the boat's number on the outside. In addition to this, each boat took to sea a variety of ready-cut

THE CREW: KEY U-BOAT POSITIONS

The electric controls of *U-889* (Type IXC/40).

metal blanks so that any other parts that might break could be replicated at sea. To get promotion in the engineering division it was necessary to have a technical qualification, so boats usually had several people on board with excellent toolmaking or metalworking backgrounds. Boats, especially the long-range types, were obviously equipped with basic tools such as drills, lathes and welding gear.

Whilst it is possible to find information about the technical aspects of engines, very few authors have succeeded in translating this into how it might have influenced the war at sea. Paul Weidlich, the engineer officer of *U-518* (Type IXC), is one of the few who has left some valuable notes in the German U-boat Museum about the performance of his boat. From theses one can work out that a U-boat travelling on the surface for more than about 23 hours per day could cover from about 120–170nm per day, depending on the force of the winds and currents. During this period the boat would consume between about 2.0–3.5 tons of fuel, while the men used between 200–270 litres of drinking water. For anyone wanting more detailed figures, a summary of his log is included as Appendix 3.

The sound-retarding door between the diesel compartment and the electric motor-cum-after torpedo room of *U-995*. The incredible sound of machinery running inside a submarine is unimaginable unless one has experienced it and even special soundproof doors only took some of the edge off the noise and it was still impossible to carry on a normal conversation anywhere near the diesels.

THE CREW: KEY U-BOAT POSITIONS

Above and below: The electric controls of *U-534* (Type IXC/40) at the Woodside Ferry Terminal (Birkenhead).

Above and left: *U-995* (Type VIIC) at Laboe near Kiel (Germany) showing the electric controls. Looking backwards from the door leading to the diesel compartment. The rear torpedo tube with an open door is visible in the distance. The machine towards the left next to the torpedo tube is an air compressor. The main electric motors protrude slightly above the level of the deck, with enough space between them calculated to accommodate one torpedo.

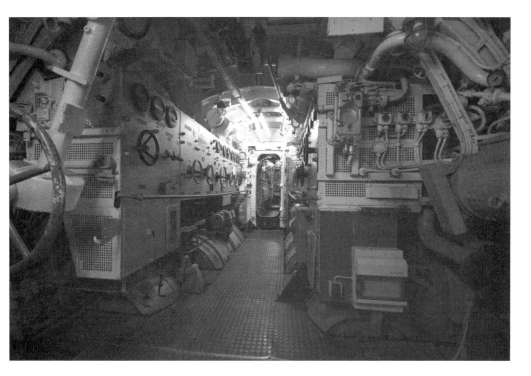

Above and right: The rear torpedo compartment with electric controls of *U-955*, looking from astern towards the diesel compartment with emergency steering wheel just visible towards the left in its folded-away position.

The diesel mechanic is holding the throttle with his left hand and the starting lever in his right.

THE CREW: KEY U-BOAT POSITIONS

What the diesel mechanic is looking at – the main diesel controls.

At the top, towards the left is the circular engine telegraph with a wheel to shut off the main air duct. Behind the hand wheel attached to the ceiling are a set of rectangular indicators showing the temperature of each cylinder inside the engine and a seventh for the exhaust pipe. With so many pipes and ducts running into and out of the engine room meant that there was an abundance of taps, wheels and levers for closing them when it became necessary.

Inset: The engine telegraph with a revolution counter towards the left.

The diesel compartment of a Type IX boat. There was an escape hatch above the man on the right.

The diesel compartment of a Type II, with hardly any room around the engine for maintenance work. Many of the earlier engines were open at the top where the various rockers and their associated gear were constantly moving when the engine was running. The moving parts were then lubricated manually.

THE CREW: KEY U-BOAT POSITIONS

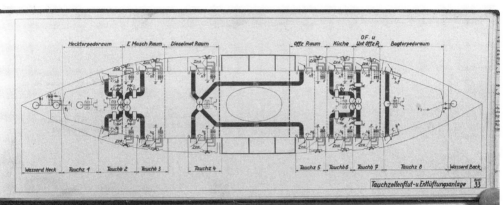

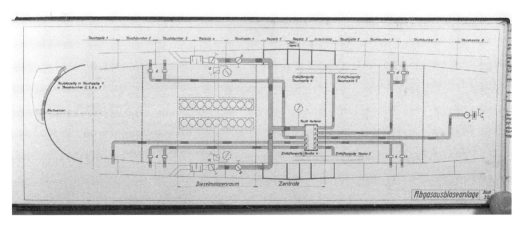

Mechanics were expected to know the arrangements and setting of the frequently-used machinery and they had special pocket-sized hardbound books for tracing all manner of pipes that they might only have to deal with occasionally during emergencies. This is one such book containing diagrams.

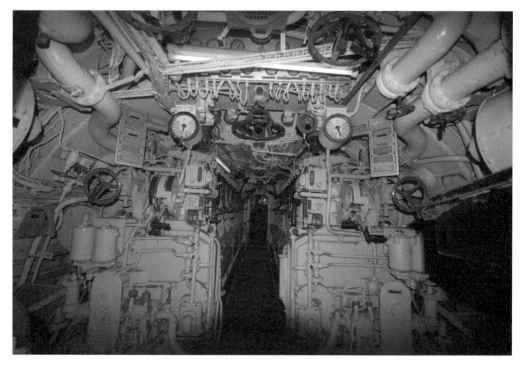

The diesel engines of *U-995* looking aft towards the door leading to the stern torpedo compartment with the electric controls beyond.

A close up of *U-995*'s diesel engines looking forward.

THE CREW: KEY U-BOAT POSITIONS

Above: The diesel engines looking forward with the large red clutch wheels in the foreground.

Right: The diesel compartment of *U-534*.

The forward end of the *U-534*'s diesel compartment with workbenches and a vice in the foreground.

The diesel compartment of *U-534*.

Cook (*Smut*)

Napoleon's famous words that an army marches on its stomach had been well digested by the time the Second World War started and U-boat men were provided with the best provisions available. The cook

The German word for cook is *Koch*, but aboard ships he tends to be known officially as *Smut* or *Smutje*. On Type VII boats the galley was situated immediately forward of the diesel compartment, meaning that the noise from this area was constantly in the cook's ears and the fumes that leaked out when the door was opened added their unique flavour to whatever food was within reach.

Above left: The man on the right is facing his tiny stove with a large pot on it.

Above right: Facing in the other direction – that is forward – the cook had a small work surface and sink with four taps. These provided (from left to right) washing water, filtered drinking water, warm seawater and drinking water. The large wheel behind the cook's head is part of the most important part of any U-boat's equipment, a coffee grinder, and came in a variety of different shapes and sizes. The man has a towel wrapped around his waist instead of an apron and the navy made pilfering difficult by having its name woven into the material. Drinking water was usually supplied via a hosepipe from a tap while fresh washing water came from a larger fire hydrant, but both were supplied through the same water main.

responsible for preparing the food did not stand normal watches. Instead he was expected to keep the men fed without regard to what else might be going on and there were many cases where hardened crews were not put out of action by seasickness. So dealing with large cooking pots during storms became a real balancing act to prevent the contents from enriching the floor. The galley hatch served as the main entrance when in port. Then the galley was often shut down because the men were provided with meals from canteens on shore.

Radio Operators

The golden rule for all radio operators was that thoroughness was more important than speed and there were long lists of directives to ensure everything followed the correct order as laid down in the naval regulations. These rules were so stringent and the wording so precise that they became a great aid for cryptanalysts at Bletchley Park when breaking the secret U-boat radio code.

At first the majority of leading radio operators were petty officers, but by the time the war started a good number had already been promoted to warrant officers with sword knot. Besides sending, receiving and coding messages, the radio officer also doubled up as hydrophone operator when submerged and many were also qualified as paramedics. The radio room was also a hub for the boat's own loudspeaker system, making it

Radio operators were not allowed to remove the headsets from their ears while on duty and often had a number of other jobs in addition to dealing with radios. The panel on the bulkhead behind the men contained a large number of fuses. The circular heads of these could be unscrewed and a new fuse inside a ceramic fitting inserted. (German fuses consisted of small bottle-shaped ceramic fittings with the appropriate wire inside them. So it was a case of throwing away the old ones and merely screwing a new one into the box rather than having to fiddle with small pieces of wire.)

possible to broadcast announcements, live radio or music from a record player as directed by the commander. It was not unusual for boats going on long voyages to take several hundred records with them.

The main operator was usually not allowed to remove his headphones while on duty, although some boats ignored this regulation when they were in positions where they could not pick up incoming signals. Coding and sending or receiving messages required a team of three men. One

The metal corners on the lapels indicate that this is a petty officer, probably the chief radio operator, and the earphones suggest he happens to be on duty. While waiting for messages radio operators often typed out a good copy of the handwritten logbook. It would be possible to fill several volumes with just radio equipment, but the subject is rather complicated and the majority of people are hardly likely to be inspired by the technology involved. Yet, at a most basic level, it is important to bear in mind that this was all rather sensitive gear working with large glass valves instead of tiny robust transistors and a depth charge could easily put these delicate instruments out of action. The German U-boat Museum in Cuxhaven-Altenbruch is in the process of recreating a U-boat radio room with authentic equipment and it is also possible to find some interesting communications equipment at Bletchley Park in Milton Keynes (England). A search on the Internet will also reveal a large number of radio enthusiasts with in-depth knowledge to explain what all the magic boxes were used for.

A radio kept for emergencies aboard Type VIIC U-boats.

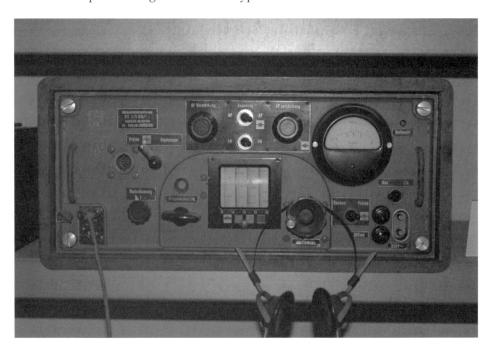

The receiver for the FuMB 4 radar detector (*Samos*).

THE CREW: KEY U-BOAT POSITIONS

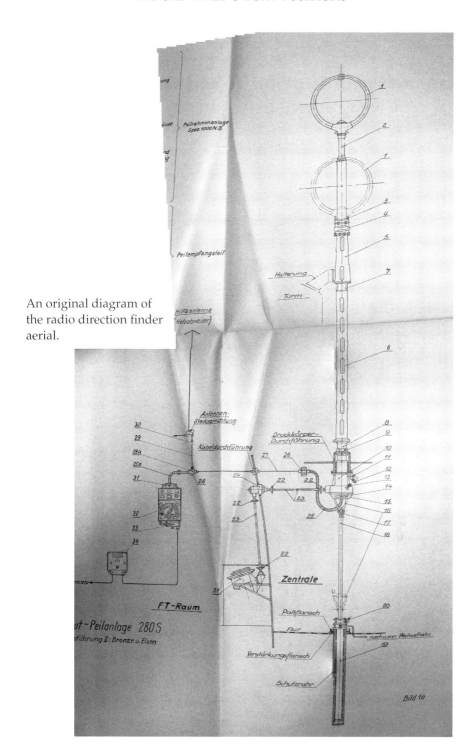

An original diagram of the radio direction finder aerial.

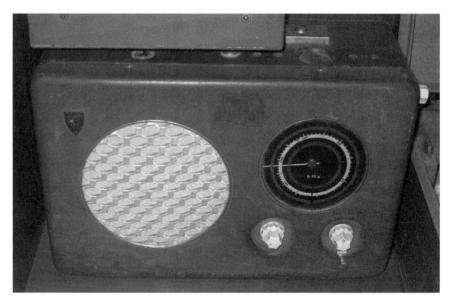

A common or garden radio as the men might have had at home, but in a simplified box for entertaining the crew and listening to civilian radio stations. The white knobs below the dial were put there after the original ones had been stolen long after the end of the war.

man would press the keys of the Enigma machine while another wrote down the letter that illuminated above the keyboard and a third man then transmitted the message. Often the traffic allowed for one man to be receiving and sending messages while the other two concentrated on the coding process. Of course, there were also times when two men coded messages waiting to be transmitted and then one of the two sent them off when conditions allowed. The problem with this was that the code changed every day and messages could not be left in the coded state for too long.

The large deck gun, situated immediately above the radio room, sometimes worked wonders with delicate radio equipment, and depth charges could also make radios go on strike. Even when not aggravated, radios were still the most 'temperamental' part of any submarine, which meant that checks and maintenance work occupied a good part of each day. It was possible for submerged U-boats off America to pick up signals from Germany, but they also had periscopic-rod aerials to improve reception and transmissions while at sea. Each boat would have had several radio sets plus some emergency equipment for when the main system was out of order. Special visual reporting stations for boats that returned with damaged radios were located near the main bases.

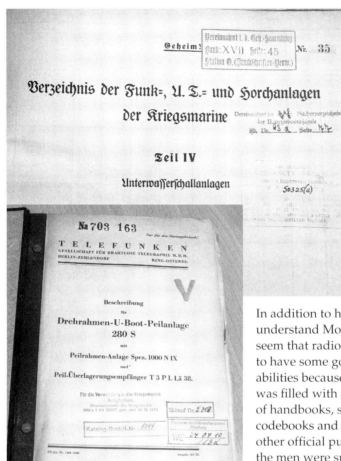

In addition to having to understand Morse, it would seem that radio operators had to have some good reading abilities because this small area was filled with a vast variety of handbooks, study books, codebooks and all manner of other official publications that the men were supposed to read when there was nothing important going on.

Left: The radio operator also doubled up as operator for the sound detection gear for which there was a special compartment forward of the radio room.

Below: Sending messages for the radio direction finder was an easy matter of finding the right code of the day, usually consisting of only a few letters of Morse code. The person at the receiving end had a more complicated job. First he had to isolate the signal on the right frequency for the direction finder and then rotate the aerial until he obtained the best possible sound to determine the direction it is coming from. One advantage that no longer features on modern radios is that many of the better-quality old sets had a 'magic eye' to provide a visual indication of the signal strength.

Torpedo Mechanics

The engineer officer was ultimately responsible for all matters concerning torpedoes, but he delegated the daily routine work to the senior torpedo mechanic, who was always a warrant officer and the only person of such rank to sleep with the men in the bow compartment.

Above and right: In a submarine no one could get further away from the commander and irritating watch officers than the torpedo mechanics. To make sure that the hierarchy did not have to follow the 'Lords' into the crowded and depressingly stuffy extremities, there was a telephone and a voice pipe connection. A voice pipe running through the diesel engine room would have produced a symphony of offensive background noises, but this problem didn't get in the way when communicating with the main 'attack end' at the front of the boat.

Left: This man could be holding on with his right hand to steady himself while opening the door with his left or he might be holding on with his left while he has his right is over the torpedo's trigger. Note the end of the voice pipe by his left hand.

Right: The outside torpedo doors were opened and closed by turning this handle. Each tube had its own opening mechanism.

THE CREW: KEY U-BOAT POSITIONS

Despite his seniority and having first call on what went on in that room, he was not responsible for discipline or for domestic arrangements there. The senior torpedo mechanic was supported by at least one petty officer and usually a more senior petty officer in the stern, if the compartment there had a torpedo tube. Obviously there were a good number of torpedo ratings as well.

Electric torpedoes had to be partly withdrawn from their tubes at least once every three days for charging the batteries and, in addition to this, there was also a fairly lengthy maintenance schedule that had to be checked at regular intervals. The regulations stated that reloading torpedoes or withdrawing them from their tubes for charging batteries

Adjusting the final firing settings from the bridge was done almost automatically while the torpedo was lying in the tube with the outer doors open, ready for discharge. This shows the simple device in the stern of *U-995*, where the indications from the bridge can be seen in the middle of the dial and all the torpedo mechanics had to do was to twist the wheel on the right until the pointers at the outside of the ring matched those from the bridge. The massive motor behind this unit worked the rear hydroplanes.

Torpedoes were usually delivered without detonators, which arrived with each one packed in a special tin, some of which can be seen on the left-hand side, in front of the tubes. The derrick gear for lifting torpedoes is visible near the ceiling. At the back of the photo, between the upper two tubes, is the special device for making adjustments to the later Type LUT anti-convoy torpedoes. There was also a normal torpedo-adjusting gadget near the front of the torpedo tubes, but that is not visible in this picture. Bunks would normally have been fitted in front of the lockers on each side. This shows a Type IXC U-boat, probably *U-889*.

could be carried out even in Sea States 6–7 and it was important to practise this in such weather so that the boat could maintain contact with convoys when shadowing them.

The big problem with this rule was that it was written by seasoned seamen who had taken command of land-based desks and the majority of wartime crews that followed them didn't have the experience, the sea legs nor the strong stomachs to cope with maintenance work in such extremely arduous conditions. Reloading torpedoes was another matter

THE CREW: KEY U-BOAT POSITIONS

The bow compartment of *U-995* before it was vandalised by thieving visitors.

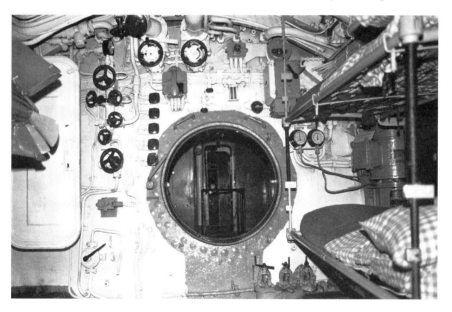

Looking aft in the bow torpedo compartment of a Type IXC. As can clearly be seen here, there was a water and pressure-resistant bulkhead with circular hatch while Type VII had a normal rectangular door in this position. The open rectangular door with round corners on the left that is half hidden by the torpedo is the heads or lavatory and there is a ballast pump on the right of the photo.

Above and opposite: The bow torpedo tubes of *U-995*.

THE CREW: KEY U-BOAT POSITIONS

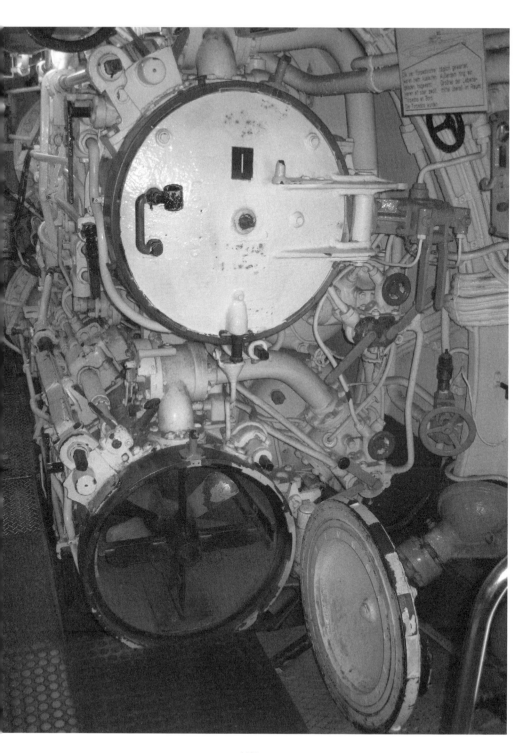

The bow torpedo tubes of *U-534*.

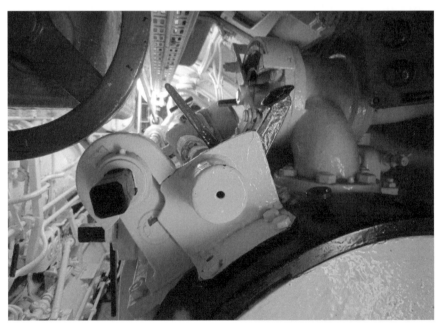

The black rectangular projection is the end of the rod that opens and closes the outside torpedo doors and the lever with the flat top towards the right is the trigger for launching the torpedo. The red stalk to its left is a safety catch. Torpedoes could be launched from both the central control room and the conning tower.

THE CREW: KEY U-BOAT POSITIONS

Right: The bow torpedo compartment of *U-995* with a G7a torpedo on the right.

Below: The stern torpedo tube of *U-995* with an air compressor on the left.

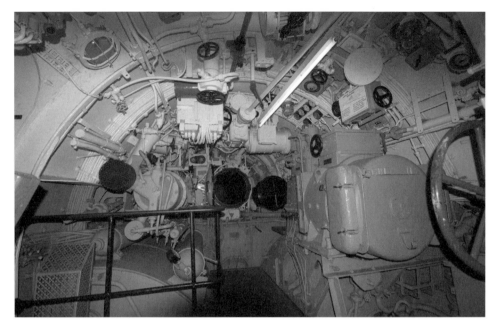

Above and below: U-995, looking aft from the electric control panel.

THE CREW: KEY U-BOAT POSITIONS

The torpedo detonator that could have been set off either by the contact levers or by the magnetic field of the target had to be adjusted before discharging it. These vital pieces of the torpedo were supplied packed in a special protective tin container and were screwed into the torpedo once it was inside the U-boat. This one is on display at the *U-534* Museum in Birkenhead.

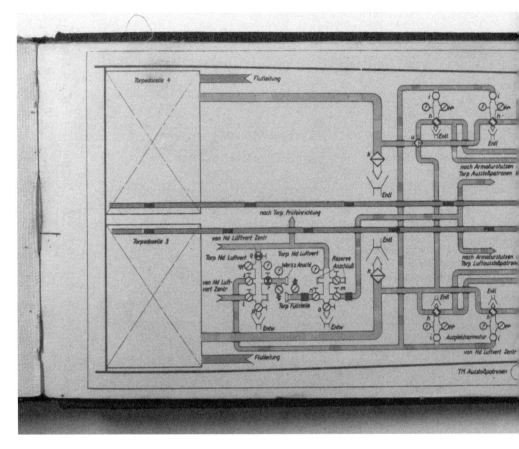

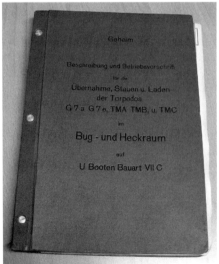

Torpedo handbook and plan of the pipework used for flooding the bow torpedo tubes.

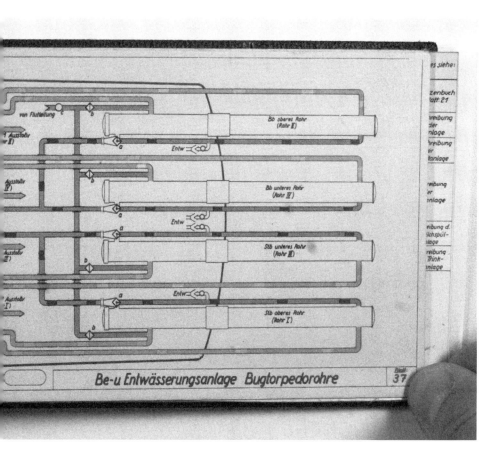

and could not be carried out during rough weather because the heavy torpedo was winched up while suspended by a couple of chains and these would have allowed it to swing violently when the waves were too fierce. Dealing with an emergency dive during such a precarious situation would also have been suicidal. The engineer officer could well have lost control of the boat.

Withdrawing torpedoes from their tubes or moving the heavy handling apparatus could only be done with the engineer officer's permission while he was on duty. It was the First Watch Officer's duty to work through the entire torpedo-firing schedule with the senior torpedo mechanic at the beginning of each day to check that everything was functioning properly. This check also served as a training session for the men concerned and was important enough for the First Officer to report the completion of the task to the commander.

The U-boat's Nerve Centre: The Central Control Room

The Central Control Room
(Looking forward and to starboard)
1. Officers' accommodation.
2. Sound and radio room.
3. Hatch door.
4. Diving controls.
5. Port engine telegraph – the starboard telegraph is slightly to the right.
6. Position of where the slave unit of the gyrocompass used to be.
7. End of illuminated periscope to see the magnetic compass.
8. Steering controls.
9. Speaking pipe to bridge.
10. Loudspeaker.
11. Rudder position indicator.

12. Canisters for removing carbon dioxide from the air.
13. Navigation periscope.
14. Depth gauge up to 25m.
15. Bow hydroplane control – stern control to the right.
16. Periscope depth indicator. (A complicated manometer named *Papenberg* in U-boats after the person who first introduced them.)
17. Engine revolution and direction indicator.
18. Indicator showing position of hydroplanes.
19. Trimming panel.
20. Compressed-air bottles.

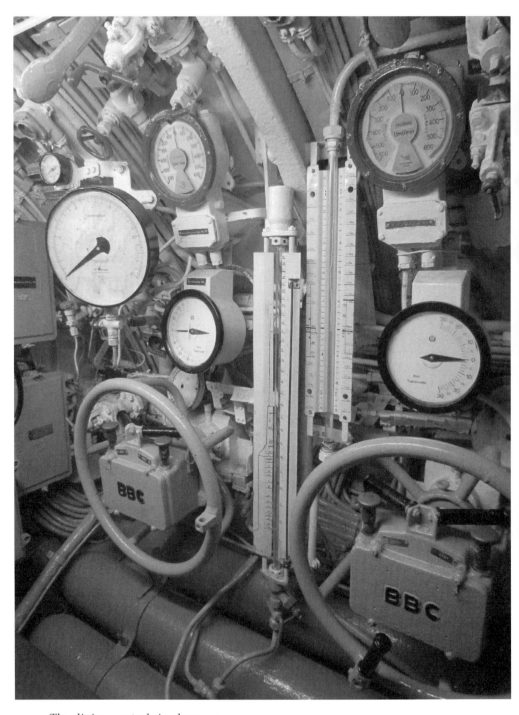

The diving controls in close-up.

THE CREW: KEY U-BOAT POSITIONS

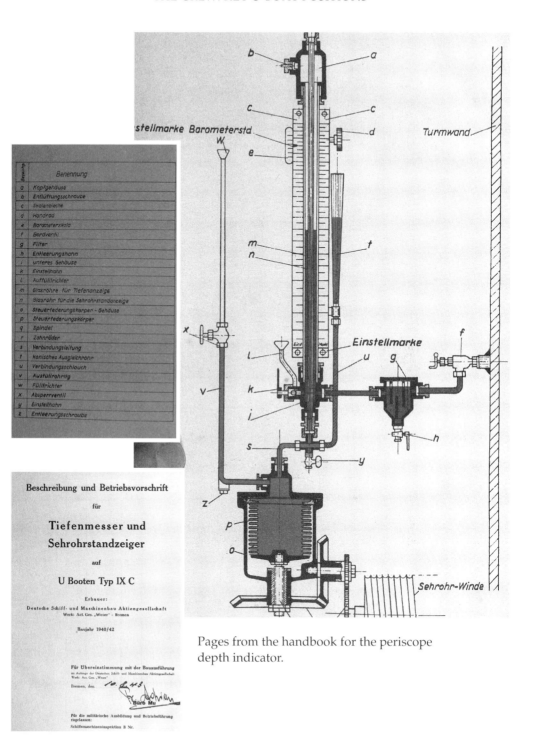

Pages from the handbook for the periscope depth indicator.

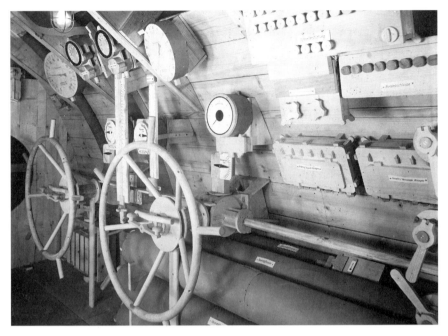

Above and opposite: The wooden hydroplane controls for the large Type XI that was never built. Before laying down a new U-boat type, the dockyard built a life-size version out of wood, to assure that the individual components fitted into the design.

The vents of diving tanks and the closures of air ducts were operated by heavily geared hand wheels or by levers in the ceiling, which are in use in this photograph.

THE CREW: KEY U-BOAT POSITIONS

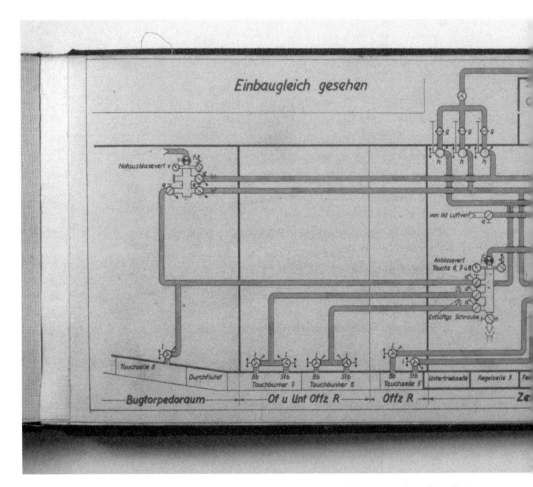

A page from a handbook showing the emergency blowing tubes for diving cells.

THE CREW: KEY U-BOAT POSITIONS

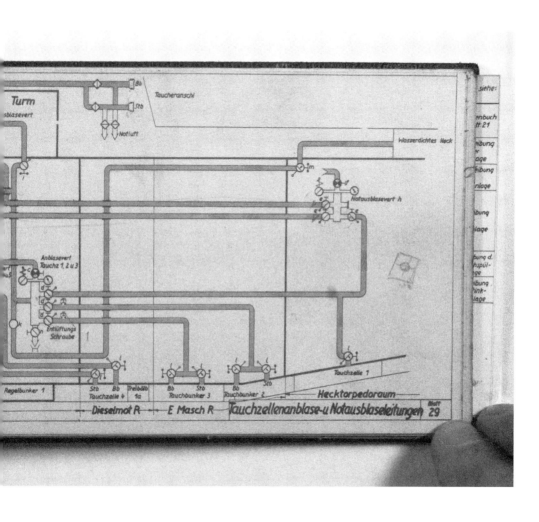

Above and opposite: The trimming panel to the right of the hydroplane controls. Very few men were allowed to touch these controls and those that had to handle the taps had to be able to find the right one in total darkness. This so-called 'Christmas Tree' controlled the balance of the boat, so that it sat comfortably in the water when dived and it was necessary to make adjustments every time heavy weights were moved. A man walking from one end of the boat to the other was enough to upset the balance, so this gear was a vitally important part of operations.

THE CREW: KEY U-BOAT POSITIONS

The trimming panel in *U-995*.

Above and overleaf: One of the big ballast pumps at the rear of the central control room with inspection covers for various pipes that run through this part of the boat. The cover from one of these pipes leading to the outside was removed and thrown onto the deck when *U-505* was evacuated. An American sailor found it, guessed that its absence was responsible for filling the place with water and replaced it to prevent the boat from sinking. U-boats also carried scuttling charges with a time fuse that could be placed near vital pipes to blow them open. During the early days of the war some U-boats used these for sinking ships they had stopped to save their valuable torpedoes for more difficult targets.

HITLER'S ATTACK U-BOATS

THE CREW: KEY U-BOAT POSITIONS

Above and right: The duty watch usually consisted of four lookouts plus one officer and it was necessary for the men to report every five minutes or so that they had seen nothing of importance. Although officers were expected to know Morse code and semaphore, many hardly ever used these methods for communication and the majority could only do so at a slow rate. In addition to the duty watch a signalman would be on hand somewhere to be called up to the top of the conning tower when it was necessary to exchange visual messages.

Above and below: A number of differently-coloured flares and at least one signal pistol were always kept ready inside the conning tower. Such guns were supplied by a number of different makers, meaning a variety of different designs were in use.

THE CREW: KEY U-BOAT POSITIONS

The duty watch with the torpedo sight's binoculars clipped in place. The lookouts are wearing rubber raincoats and sou'westers while the rest of the attacking crew has appeared without protection from the weather, but they are wearing lifejackets, suggesting they might be standing by to man the deck gun.

The crew for the 88mm deck gun in position. Although the container at the front of the boat has been opened, it would seem likely that this is an exercise because a commander would hardly have allowed an extra man with a camera to climb on deck during a real attack.

Once in port it was necessary for each boat to provide its own sentries and these could usually be identified because they carried some kind of weapon, even if it was only a bayonet on a belt while inside the well-protected U-boat bunkers. Guards were not allowed to sit or lounge by leaning against the superstructure. This shows Matrosengefreiter Müller standing in front of a 37mm anti-aircraft gun.

THE CREW: KEY U-BOAT POSITIONS

Some deactivated examples of sidearms carried by U-boats.

Pages 175-178: It was unlikely that U-boat men could identify every ship they were likely to spot on the high seas, so they were issued with handbooks showing the most likely vessels they might meet. Many U-boats also carried lists of merchant ships with drawings for easier identification.

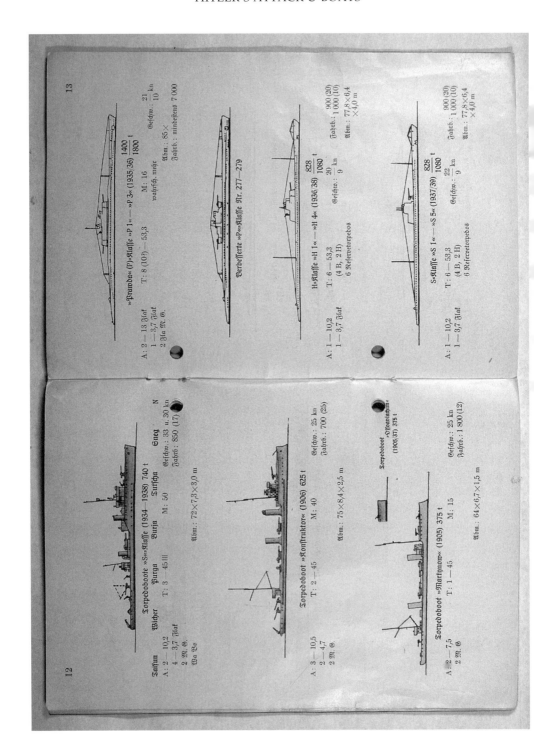

THE CREW: KEY U-BOAT POSITIONS

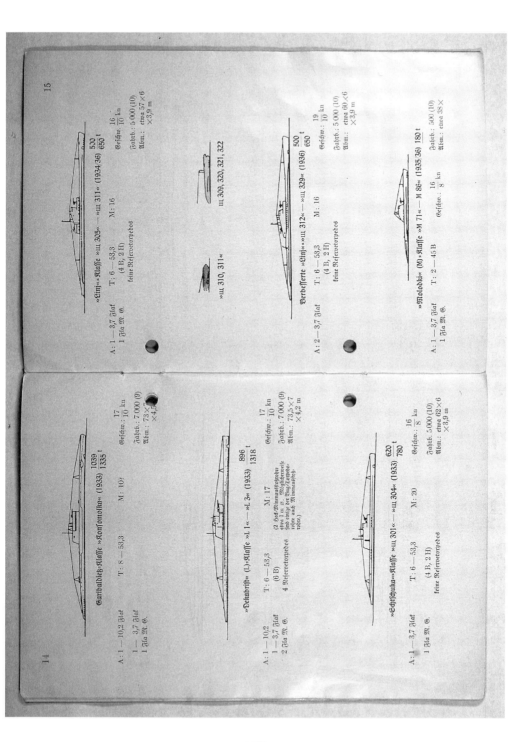

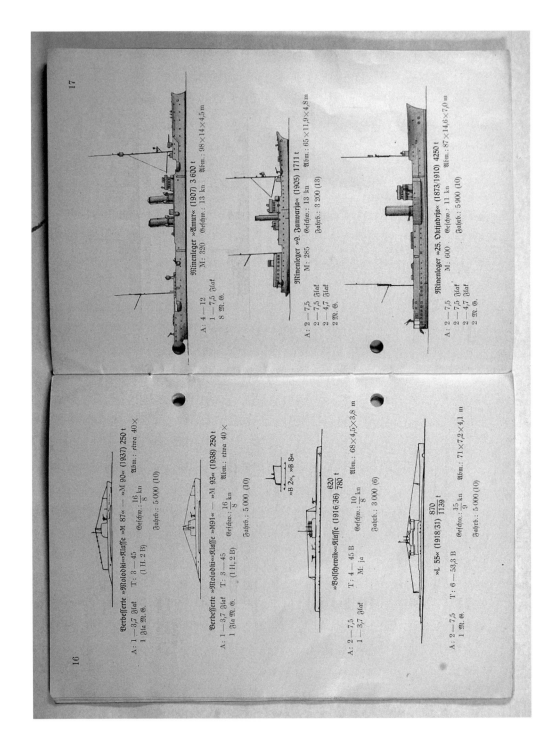

THE CREW: KEY U-BOAT POSITIONS

Ober~steuer~mann (Navigator)

The Navigator or *Ober~steuer~mann* must not be confused with the helmsman. He did not steer the boat. A warrant officer with sword knot, who had risen from the ranks and therefore had some ten years of experience behind him, nearly always occupied this position. In port he dealt with the storing of provisions and once at sea he was responsible for navigation, meaning he had to have good mental arithmetic abilities because during the Second World War there were no significant calculators to help him with quite complicated number-crunching. This was so important that although he doubled up as Third Watch Officer, he was relieved of this duty as soon as a chase started so that he could concentrate on the navigation. The commander and *Ober~steuer~mann* were the only men allowed to mark anything on the navigation chart.

The regulations stated that the navigator had to take every opportunity to shoot the sun and stars with as many people as possible so that all the results could be compared to assure that the positions calculated were correct. Especially during poor conditions every change of engine

Above left: *Ober~steuer~mann* Kleyer of *U-9*.

Above right: *Ober~steuer~mann* Dahlmann of *U-108* (on the left) with his distinctive and most elaborate shoulder straps. This person was a warrant officer with swordknot and wore a peaked cap without braiding. The woollen bobble hat on the right was not a present from granny but proper naval issue for men working outside on open decks.

Above left: Ober~steuer~mann Haupt of U-203.

Above right: Shooting the sun or the stars was such an important part of the daily routine that several men were sent up to do this so that the results could be compared to make sure that an as-near-as-possible correct reading had been taken. Sextants were personal property for men in the merchant navy but not in the Kriegsmarine where ships were supplied with a number of different models. Some of them were manual as can be seen here, but later in the war the navy also produced models with a gyroscope to make things easier and quicker when the waves were not cooperative. Towards the beginning of the war shooting the sun or stars was a leisurely affair but towards the end air attacks became so frequent that many attempts were frustrated and men had to work exceedingly quickly if they were going to get a reading at all.

revolution, speed indicator and compass heading were recorded, which at times added up to a long list of figures. These had to be checked every four hours with magnetic compass, gyrocompass and chronometer to assure that that the correct courses were marked on the chart. Once an attack started the navigation details were recorded on millimetre graph paper.

Authors have claimed that the *Steuer~mann* was nicknamed 'Karl' in many boats, which is not true. It would seem that this came about

THE CREW: KEY U-BOAT POSITIONS

Above left: Feldwebel or Sergeants were often also referred to as Chief Petty Officers in Britain, but there was a stark difference in experience, training and uniforms between a Petty Officer (Maat) and a Warrant Officer with *Portepee* (Swordknot). After the First World War the navy recognised that the training for warrant officers was partly to blame for some poor performances and set about establishing this group as vital link in the command chain. They even produced a handbook for this key element.

Above right: Navigation within the tight confines of a submarine was such a difficult job that only the commander and the *Ober~steuer~mann* were allowed to mark anything on the chart laid out on the small table. (*Ober~steuer~mann* was the lowest rank of this trade in U-boats, which didn't employ a lower ranking *Steuer~mann* as was found in some surface ships.)

as a result of English-speaking historians not being able to understand Low German, the language that predominated in ports until well after the Second World War. Colloquially he was referred to as '*Steuer~kerl*' meaning 'Steering Bloke' rather than the official and much more polite '*Steuer~mann*'. The lowest rank of this position in a U-boat was *Ober~steuer~mann*.

Watch Officers

Although the *Ober~steuer~mann* doubled up as Third Watch Officer and usually was a warrant officer with sword knot rather than a commissioned officer, he often had far more seagoing experience than any other person in the U-boat. The statement by some American historians that warrant officer ranks were abolished after the First World War is far from correct. Being fully aware that this was one of the weak links during the First World War, the German Navy set up two special warrant officer schools (one for the Baltic and the other for the North Sea Naval Commands) and it was necessary to have served for at least several years before being allowed into them and then the men also had to sign on for somewhere in region of ten or twelve years.

The First and Second Watch Officers, usually with only three or four years of training, were there to assist the commander by taking over

U201 (Kapitänleutnant Adalbert Schnee) with the commander in the white cap and his two watch officers. The man looking towards the camera has his hand on the voice pipe leading down to the central control room. A periscope support, a magnetic sighting compass in gimbals and the top of the torpedo sight without binoculars clipped in place can be made out in the middle.

The shoulder strap of the man on the right indicates that he is an officer of the lowest rank group. In front of him is the torpedo sight with the special water and pressure-resistant binoculars clipped in position. The wooden cladding with what looks like a cooking pot on the top is the periscope. Covers were provided to prevent items and rubbish falling down the well and possibly jamming the mechanism.

the day-to-day running of the U-boat. In port they were responsible for seeing that everything was shipshape and ready for going to sea with all the stores in their correct positions. The First Watch Officer was also responsible for checking that the hatch locking mechanisms functioned properly and that the daily recognition signals were ready for use inside the conning tower. There was a framed slate, similar to those used by children in schools, for writing down the current recognition signals. In addition there should have been at least one signal pistol with ready-use flares as well. Recognition signals were often changed at least once every day.

The First Watch Officer was also responsible for making up the three watches so that the ability of the individuals was evenly spread without the most hawk-eyed men all being out at the same time. Then, when lookouts were ready for going on duty it was the officer's duty

The torpedo sight with binoculars attached and one of the watch officers. The elaborate shoulder strap of the man on right indicates that he is a warrant officer with swordknot. The emblem of two crossed anchors indicates that he is a navigator or *Steuer~mann* and the two pips indicate that he holds the more senior rank of *Ober~steuer~mann*.

to inform them how to dress. This was important. Bearing in mind that the majority of the crew were incarcerated inside a windowless U-boat, they had only the motion over the waves as a guide as to what it was like on the outside and no clue as to what weather conditions prevailed. So they had to be told what rain gear, if any, to wear and whether it was necessary to take sunglasses and so on. Then, once fully assembled on the top of the conning tower, the officer had to determine where each man should stand so that the keenest-eyed could cover the more difficult sectors. Having assessed the situation, the duty officer informed the helmsman the course he was to steer if an emergency was ordered. It was essential that the boat turned onto the course where the prevailing weather would allow it to dive as quickly as possible.

The duty officer had to make sure he knew exactly what to do and how to react to any situation that might arise. He had to take bearings on any objects sighted and report everything, including changes in the weather, to the commander. All this information was recorded in the central control room's log.

Commander

The commander was supreme ruler in each boat and ultimately responsible for everything that went on. Yet, despite this authority, many of them were open for comments and advice and some went as far as appointing a 'coward of the day' to come up with any arguments against the decisions that were taken. Both the commander and the engineer officer had to be on duty whenever any action was taken and there were times when the commander might be on duty for more than twenty-four hours. The duty officer was usually authorised to take evasive action that he considered necessary but he was not allowed

It looks highly likely that this is a small Type II U-boat because the larger boats had considerably superior facilities. There the commander sat on a saddle and he could rotate by pressing buttons with his feet. Whatever, during submerged attacks there wasn't much else for him to do other than to concentrate on the job in hand and men would have been standing by to operate the torpedo calculator and to deal with whatever he ordered. Shouting was definitely out of the question and many commanders could lead an entire attack with finger signals instead of spoken commands.

U-376 (Type VIIC) with Kapitänleutnant Friedrich-Karl Marks at the sky or navigation periscope in the central control room.

THE CREW: KEY U-BOAT POSITIONS

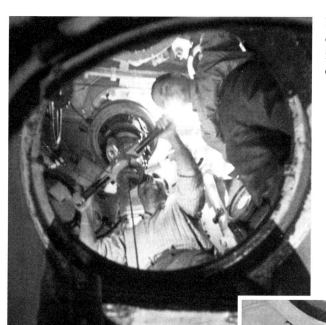

Looking up from the central control room into the conning tower compartment of a Type II.

The commander at the periscope with a chart of the approaches to the Kiel naval base on the wall.

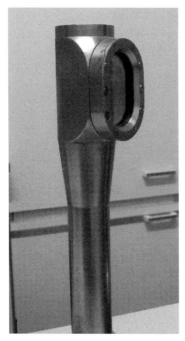

to change speed, course or do anything else without the commander being present and there were two commands for getting the commander into action. 'Commander to the bridge' allowed time for getting dressed to cope with whatever conditions prevailed outside but 'Commander to the bridge at once' meant he was to come right away

Left: The head of the attack periscope was made from stainless steel and painted grey so that it would not reflect too much light. This one has been cleaned and is on display at the German U-boat Museum in Cuxhaven-Altenbruch.

Below: Looking up into the conning tower of *U-995*.

without regard to what he might be doing or wearing. Generally nothing happened inside a U-boat without the instruction going through the commander.

Another point about commanders was that if the crew didn't like him and said so to the flotilla leader or higher authority, he was removed forthwith and there were cases of boats being delayed for a day or two while a replacement was found.

A recent error that has appeared in several books states that the German for commander was *'Kaleu'* or *'Kaleunt'*, which is not correct. The British and American address form of 'sir' does not exist in German, where people would have used the man's rank with the prefix *'Herr'* (Mr) and both these words became an accepted shortening of Kapitänleutnant. Thus 'Yes sir,' would have been *'Jawohl Herr Kaleu'*, *'Jawohl Herr Admiral*, or whatever rank was being addressed.

The commander (here Kapitänleutnant Rolf Mützelburg of *U-203*) was the first one up on the bridge when the boat surfaced and the last one down when diving, but in non-emergency situations he could delegate this responsibility to the duty officer. Clambering through the hatch was not easy. There wasn't much room.

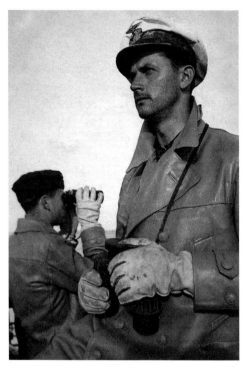

Kapitänleutnant Rolf Mützelburg of *U-203*.

It would seem that no book about submarines is complete without a picture of the commander at the periscope, but the great snag with this is that German U-boats were so small that there was hardly room to take such photographs. So some cheating was necessary or one needed an expensive camera with wide-angle lens that hardly anyone had at the time. The easiest way around the problem in a Type VII was to photograph the commander at the sky or navigation periscope that terminated inside the central control room, rather than in the commander's attack position inside the conning tower.

Watches and Operating on the Surface

The efficiency of the submarine depended very much on the discipline and ability of the duty watch. Nothing influenced the boat's readiness for action more than those few men standing on the top of the conning tower. It was strictly against naval rules for any officer to interfere with the laid-down routine and commanders were frequently told that they must not soften to improve conditions for the watch. The lookouts were a type of holy order that took priority over anything else that was going on because a large part of any success and the difference between life and death depended on them. There was usually an officer and two men facing the front plus a petty officer and one other man manning the rear. They had to report every five minutes that their sector was clear, to show that they were not losing concentration. Anything spotted had to be reported at once and the majority of boats insisted on the man pointing towards whatever he had seen. This made it easier for the officer to locate it. It was impressed upon lookouts and all other men who were in a likely position to report something approaching, not to use language that might possibly frighten the rest of the crew. So, a destroyer often became a 'fast warship' and other threatening objects had similar alternative mundane names.

Several centuries ago ships developed the custom of having two short 'dog watches' so that men did not keep the same watches every day. These were known as 'First Dog' and 'Last Dog': there never was a 'Second Dog'. Although a similar system was used on some large warships, U-boats followed a more rigid timetable with a regular twelve-hour pattern divided from 12–4, 4–8 and 8–12. This had the great advantage in a small warship that the commander knew exactly who was on duty and could arrange matters so that his best men were up top during the most difficult twilight and dawn periods. It also ensured that the First Watch Officer would be free by about 8 o'clock to deal with the checking of the torpedoes and following that check that the boat's routine was running smoothly. Strangely enough, people got very quickly accustomed to this pattern and many found it was easier than changing the sequence all the time.

Changing the watch could be quite a problem, as some boats found out to their cost by discovering that suddenly there was no one at all on the top of the conning tower. One set of men had come down and the new watch had not yet gone up. The other problem that occurred was that both the new and the old watch were on the top of the conning tower at the same time when the boat had to go into an alarm dive. Getting such a large number of men below was then quite a squash, with congestion slowing the process. To prevent such mishaps, the rules were strict, with the first man of the watch being replaced at twenty minutes before zero, the next fifteen minutes before zero and so on until everybody had been exchanged. The man coming off duty would remain up top long enough for his relief to become accustomed to the conditions. The lookouts of the duty watch changed at the designated times no matter what else was going on, whether the crew was at cruising routine or at action stations.

Some men, especially the radio operators, could find themselves in an incredibly boring situation where all they could do was to sit with the earphones on and wait for incoming messages. The regulations stated that they were not allowed to read novels but could devote the time to studying official publications, especially those suggested by the officer on duty.

Surfacing also followed a predetermined plan and in most circumstances the commander and duty watch officer would be the first up to the top of the conning tower, with the commander at the front and the other man taking the rear sector. Their first duty was to have a quick look around and then sweep the same area once again with binoculars. Only then, when everything was clear would the commander order the diesel engines to be started so that the exhaust fumes blew the majority of the tanks. While this was going on, the duty watch would also be ordered up top and then compressed air would blow the remaining water out of the tanks. Not all the tanks were connected to the diesel system.

No one was allowed onto the upper deck without the commander's permission and if any work had to be carried out then it was essential that the commander remained on the bridge until the last man was back down below. The only exception to this was during calm conditions when the duty officer could allow a few men up top for a smoke. However, naked lights were only permitted during bright conditions, otherwise the smokers had to remain inside the well-ventilated conning tower.

Each duty watch had to have a throwing rope and a lifebuoy ready in the conning tower. (Before the war these were usually hooked onto brackets on the outside of the conning tower.) There were two types, one for use during the day and another with a light for night-time. They were not so much intended as a buoyancy aid to help anyone who had fallen overboard, but to mark the spot where the lost person was likely to be. At the end of the watch, the officer would make sure that the natural-fibre rope was taken below and thoroughly dried in the engine room.

It has been claimed by some historians that U-boat commanders did not participate directly in surface attacks and usually spent the time during such action working the torpedo calculator, which is not true. It was the commander's duty to keep an overall eye on all goings-on and it was important that he should not be distracted from the overall action by focussing on only one aspect. Therefore the First Watch Officer was usually responsible for aiming and shooting torpedoes while the commander determined what to attack and how it should be approached. Under easy and calm conditions commanders could aim torpedoes and often there were trainee officers on board who were also given this job. Shooting torpedoes was relatively easy. All that had to be done was to look at the target through the special water and pressure-resistant binoculars attached to the top of the torpedo sight and then say 'fire' at the appropriate time. The vision through these binoculars was the same as all the other glasses; there was no aiming grid inside. The tricky bit of doing this was to determine angle, speed and direction of the target and then feeding the correct information into the torpedo calculator.

Engineer Officer

Although the commander was the supreme sovereign in the U-boat, there was very little that he could do without his engineer officer who had to be present for almost every manoeuvre from docking to changing positions at sea and when moving heavy objects within the submarine. It was also his duty to assure that every member of the crew had been trained to do his job properly. Many engineer officers had so much to learn that the navy provided them with what might be called 'cheating cards' for examinations. These booklets, a good number of them, contained the vital technical details necessary for the boat to function properly. Despite this, he was expected to know how to regulate the majority of operations without referral to these books. Some of the adjustments he had to make were so delicate that only he and one or two other men were allowed to even touch the necessary controls.

Leutnant zur See (Ing.) Launt of *U-365* enjoying a breath of fresh air on the top of the conning tower. He is wearing officer's shoulder straps and has a small gold-braided edge to his cap while wearing U-boat overalls that were modelled on British army battledress.

The domain of the engineer officer. As long as there were men on the bridge and a dive was imminent, he would position himself by the ladder under the hatch so that he could keep an eye on the controls and, at the same time, on what was going on above him.

U-995 looking astern along the main throughway of the central control room with the ladder leading up to the hatch in the foreground.

Like the commander and the cook, the engineer officer or LI (*Leitender Ingenieur*) did not stand normal watches. Instead he had to be on duty almost all the time and hardly any adjustments to anything were

Looking astern through the central control room from the helmsman's position. On the left is the trimming panel, in the middle the ladder leading to the top of conning tower with a voice pipe in front and the small chart table is just visible on the right. It seems likely that this is *U-889* (Type IXC/40).

allowed without the matter going through the LI. To do his work efficiently he needed a well-trained team on whom he could rely to carry out exacting work under the most difficult of conditions. To add just a few more problems, these men had to be able to find and operate the correct controls in total darkness and at times when the deck was at odd angles without anyone knowing exactly in which direction the surface of the water was likely to be. What's more, these men had to perform their exacting duties at a time when they had been severely beaten about by being thrown against hard protrusions and when the air contained so little oxygen that a carbon-dioxide count indicated life was no longer possible under such stuffy conditions.

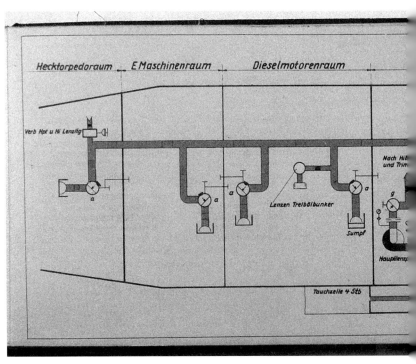

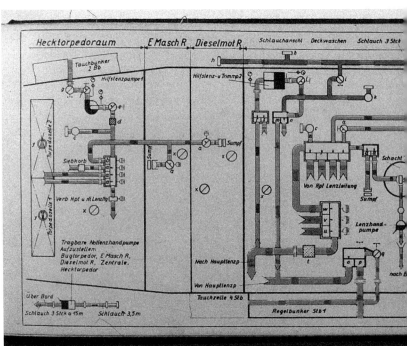

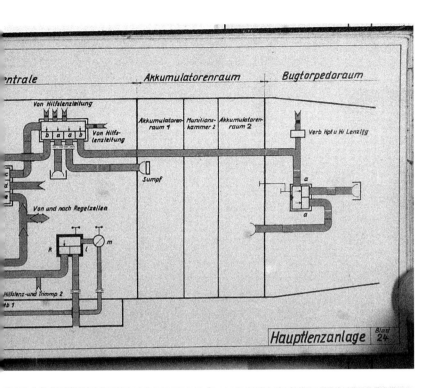

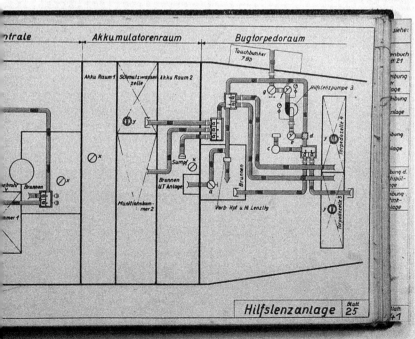

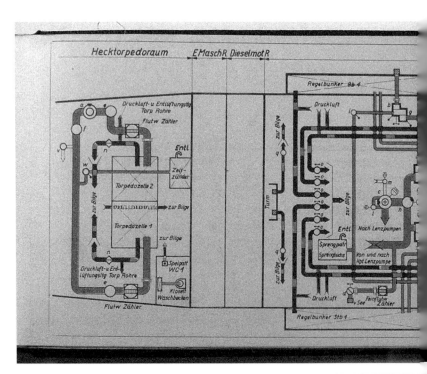
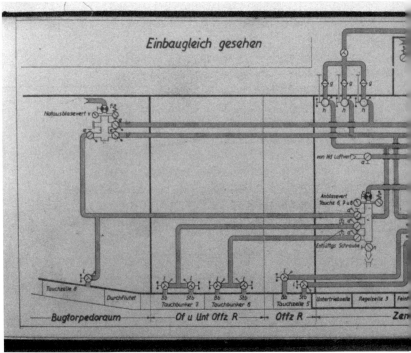

THE CREW: KEY U-BOAT POSITIONS

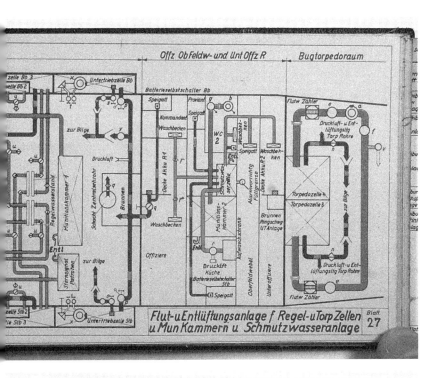

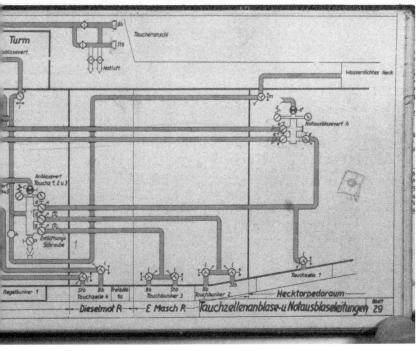

HITLER'S ATTACK U-BOATS

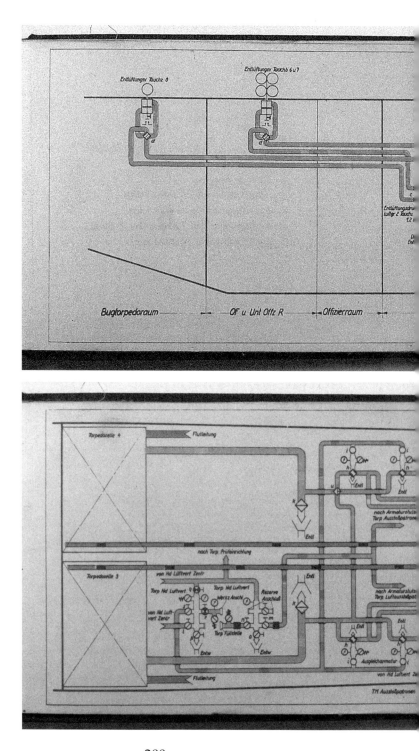

THE CREW: KEY U-BOAT POSITIONS

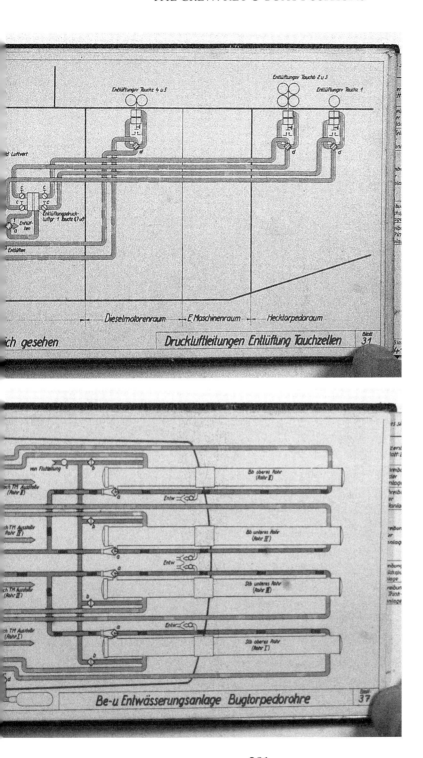

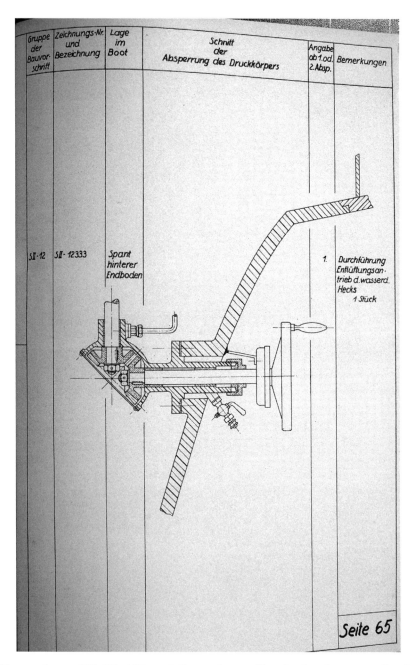

Above and pages 196-201: Although the engineer officer had such a vast collection of official publications that he was in a good position to open a bookshop, he wouldn't have found many customers because his bedtime reading was so complicated that even many seasoned U-boat men wouldn't have understood it.

Submerged Cruising – The Domain of the Engineer Officer

Once the boat dived everybody and everything had to remain calm and the hydroplanes director (a petty officer) was responsible for assuring that everything was quiet throughout the boat. On the surface orders were often shouted or passed on by whistle, which was not allowed once the boat was under the water. Then orders were whispered or passed on by hand signals. The radio operator remained at his post, keeping his headphones over his ears because even off the eastern seaboard of the United States it was still possible to receive messages when all aerials were submerged. One of the radio operators would automatically man the hydrophones as soon as the boat had left the surface. It was also common practice to reduce the power output from the batteries, which reduced the intensity of the lighting. Torches were kept ready, even when the boat was on the surface on a bright day and the position of these had to be checked as soon as the diving procedure started. They had to be found immediately in total darkness.

The order 'alarm' was even more critical than 'action stations' because so much happened so quickly during a short period of time that it was easy to dive into destruction. It would appear that this was one of the contributing reasons why only two Type I U-boats were produced. Konteradmiral Eberhard Godt, who commanded *U-25* before the war, said there were times when it was exceedingly difficult for the engineer officer to determine exactly where 'down to the centre of the earth' was and for brief periods an inexperienced man might lose sight of the exact downward angle. With men coming down from the conning tower and other perhaps not at their diving stations, there was ample opportunity for a deadly chaos to take control at this critical period and therefore many commanders took the opportunity of practising such diving sequences, even when they could rely on the crew carrying out the correct procedure.

Driving the U-boat

A man walking from one end of a submerged submarine to the other could upset the balance or trim. Therefore heavy objects could not be moved without the engineer officer's permission and he had to be on duty in the central room for the majority of manoeuvres. As soon as a boat was in deep enough water after coming out of harbour and at frequent intervals, especially after heavy objects had been moved, the boat would go into a trim or balancing dive where the engineer officer, or one of the few men who were allowed to touch the trimming panel, would adjust the water in the trim tanks. There were two halves of these at each end of the boat. One half was pumped up with compressed air so that when a tap was opened in the central control room the water would quietly be blown into the tank at the other end of the boat without having to run a noisy motor pump. Each tap had a slightly different handle to make this possible. There were also a set of regulating tanks on each side of the boat, roughly in line with the conning tower to correct any lean that might have arisen due to more weights on one side than the other.

Torpedo tubes had what were called either 'compensating' or 'torpedo' tanks near them which could be filled with seawater when torpedoes were discharged. Bearing in mind that each torpedo weighed about 1.5 tonnes about 1.5m^3 of water were required to balance out the sudden loss of the weight. There were many occasions during submerged attacks where the men didn't quite get this right and the submarine appeared briefly on the surface before returning to its correct submerged position.

A submerged submarine did not blow air into its diving tanks in order to surface. Water pressure gets less as one rises so the air inside the tanks would expand as the pressure got less and therefore result in an uncontrollable upward movement. In an emergency this might be the only way to save the crew before the submarine dropped down for good, but generally the submerged submarine was controlled in roughly the same way as an aircraft and the hydroplanes were used to bring it up to periscope depth. From there it was possible for the forward motion over the hydroplanes to bring the top of the pressure hull up as far as the surface so that the top of the conning tower was sticking up in the air. At that stage the diesel engines could be used for exhaust fumes to blow as much water as possible out of the diving tanks. Once fully on the surface, trimmed for quick diving, it was possible to blow still more water out of the tanks to raise the boat higher, but this was done only when torpedo-loading hatches had to be opened or the boat was in safe waters. The majority of tanks were open to the sea at the bottom and the sea around started to bubble when the men were too generous with the air that they were blowing into the tanks. Not all tanks had a connection to the engine room, so compressed air always remained as a vital ingredient of the diving process.

There were stabilising tanks at both ends of the boat and a set of regulating bunkers on each side of the conning tower. These could be adjusted to lift the boat high out of the water or to trim it with upper deck just below the surface of the water, ready for diving. However, in such a condition with the boat so low in the water things became rather dangerous and this was only done during calm conditions to hide the boat. There always was the possibility that the boat could easily drop down on its own accord, as happened to more than one crew. The men left swimming usually didn't like such a state of affairs.

Boats usually had specialists for every job and these 'action men' would take their positions whenever hectic conditions demanded it. The boss in the central control room was the engineer officer, but it was possible for him to be called away for emergencies elsewhere, so a number of petty officers were responsible for assuring that the controls, as ordered by the engineer officer, continued running smoothly. There was also an engineer petty officer stationed in the central control room and another petty officer was responsible for both discipline and organisation of this vital compartment.

The Helmsman

Steering a submarine on a straight course was no easy job and although each boat had a number of men capable of taking these controls, there was usually only one action helmsman for when things got really tricky. For most of the time a massive motor that was controlled by two buttons under the helmsman's hands moved the rudders. There were also two handles that he could grab to steady himself when wave motion was too rough. The two buttons fitted neatly under his wrists. The huge slave unit from the gyrocompass that was situated right in front of him indicated the boat's correct course. The helmsman could also check that the gyro was correct by glancing up at the magnetic compass through an illuminated periscope. This compass was located outside in a bulge at the front of the conning tower, which was made from non-magnetic phosphor-bronze.

When supply U-boats became a vital part of operations a considerable number of transfers had to be abandoned because attack U-boats could not steer a straight course while maintaining a constant speed. So, steering and controlling submarines could not have been easy matter.

Above and opposite: The helmsman of what looks like a Type VII U-boat.

THE CREW: KEY U-BOAT POSITIONS

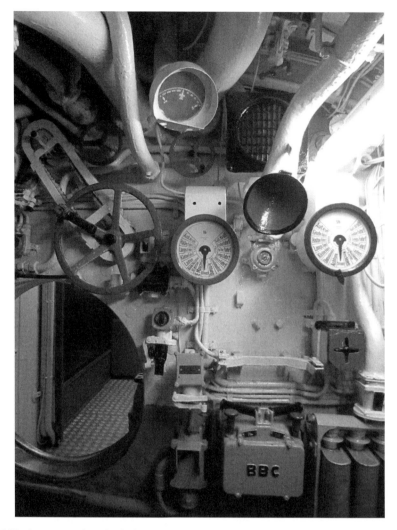

U-995, showing what the helmsman was looking at, except that his main steering guide, the slave unit from the gyrocompass, is missing. It used to occupy the empty space between the two engine telegraphs. Between them is the voice pipe leading up to the top of the conning tower and the illuminated magnetic compass is visible at the top, to the left of the loudspeaker. Note that this is in a different position to the photo showing the helmsman in action. The tins to the right of the rudder controls on the Brown Boveri & Co. (BBC) box contained potash for absorbing carbon dioxide for keeping the air clean during long dives. These were added towards the end of the war. Earlier during the war each man would have strapped one of these tins to his chest. A rubber pipe connected it to a mouthpiece. There were hand wheels and levers in the ceiling for controlling the airflow into the interior and for adjusting the levels in the outside tanks.

The Emergency Steering Wheel

The helmsman had no alternative controls to the electrical system of pressing the two buttons and this entire system failed if depth charges blew the fuses or broke wires. Since this would have been catastrophic, an alternative manual steering wheel was provided at the rear of the stern compartment. This wheel was hinged at the top so that it could be pushed out of the way when it was not required. Getting information from the bridge to the men operating this wheel was not easy and during training U-boats had to continue steering correct courses while the orders were passed on from man to man through the noisy engine room with the diesels running at such high speed that no one could hear themselves shout.

U-505 (Type IXC) in the Science and Industry Museum of Chicago, showing the stern compartment with bunks made up and with the emergency wheel in steering position in front of the two torpedo tubes.

The emergency steering wheel as seen by its operator, with the supporting bar towards the left, holding it in place.

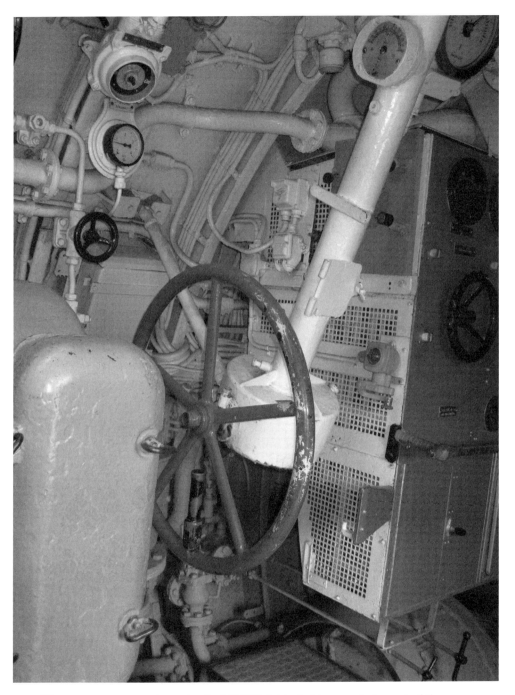

The emergency steering wheel of *U-995*, folded sideways to be out of the way when not in use.

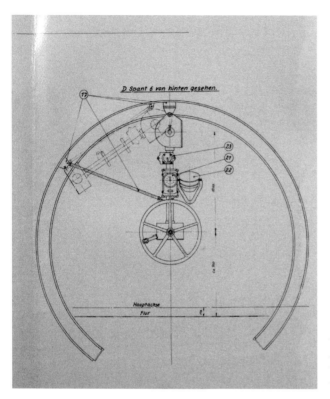

Left, below and opposite: A wartime diagram of the emergency steering wheel.

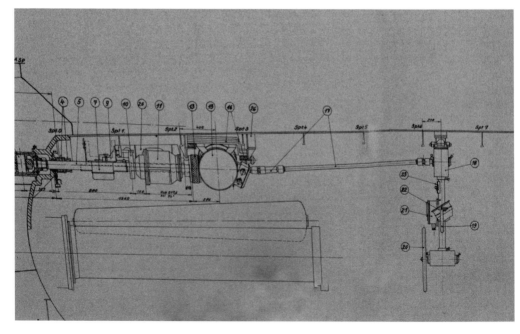

THE CREW: KEY U-BOAT POSITIONS

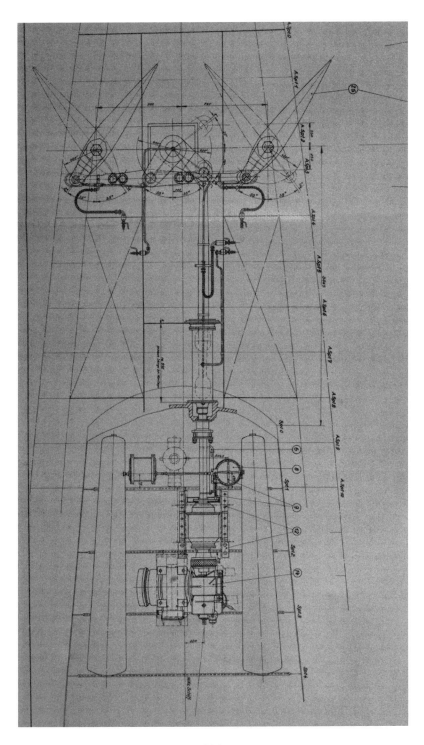

The Hydroplane Operators

It would appear that all German attack U-boats of the Second World War had their diving controls on the starboard (right-hand) side, so that the man on the left controlled the forward and man on the right the stern hydroplanes. Each set functioned independently of the other and the engineer officer would order the necessary adjustments that had to be made. It would seem that the alarm dive order was about the only action that could be triggered without the LI (engineer officer) having to give the correct orders and the reason for this running automatically

The stern hydroplane operator in what looks like a Type VII U-boat.

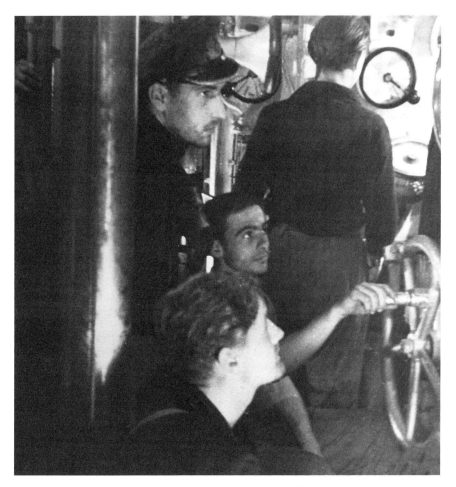

The hydroplanes of the smaller Type II were originally all manual without any powered assistance.

was that those emergency settings were always the same in each boat. In any case, even if the LI was off duty in the heads, he was likely to be back in central room before the last man came tumbling down from the bridge and he would still oversee the mechanical performance.

Unlike the helmsman, the two hydroplane operators had two ways of making adjustments. First, the usual way was to use the electrical box similar to that, which controlled the rudder's motor. Around this was the alternative system, controlled by a large steel wheel that had to be turned manually with muscle power. These wheels were connected to the front and back by thick iron rods joined in several places by universal joints that allowed the straight rods to negotiate bends.

The strange point is that these control rods crossed over within the hull to link with the hydroplanes on the starboard side. There was one more system for controlling the hydroplanes if this manual system failed. There was a well on the inside of the pressure hull where the hydroplane rod passed through. This cavity was just large enough for a man to crawl into. Down there was another manual wheel and a set of necessary gauges for making adjustments. These were also fitted with a depth gauge and these positions were always manned when action stations sounded.

Some non-German submarines were fitted with large spirit levels to indicate the angle of the submerged boat. The Germans used a dial that consisted of a rod with a weight at the bottom swinging over a protractor.

Life Inside the U-Boat: Gems in Little-Known Museums

It would seem that the story of *U-534* having been cut into sections and set up as a museum at the Woodside Ferry Terminal (Birkenhead) is reasonably well known, but the intriguing fact that

this also houses something far more exciting seems to have remained secret. There is also a display of items recovered from the wreck. The amazing thing about this is that so much, including sheets of paper and thin textiles have remained in such incredibly good condition while lying on the bottom of the sea for such a long time. It would seem that this is now the only museum in the world that throws a fascinatingly deep light into how the men lived inside a U-boat under such arduous war conditions. The following photographs show part of that completely unique display.

THE CREW: KEY U-BOAT POSITIONS

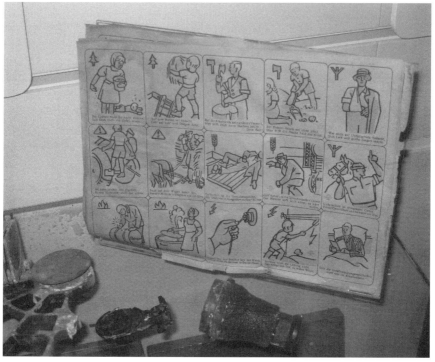

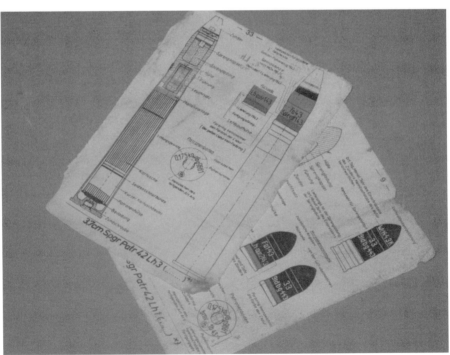

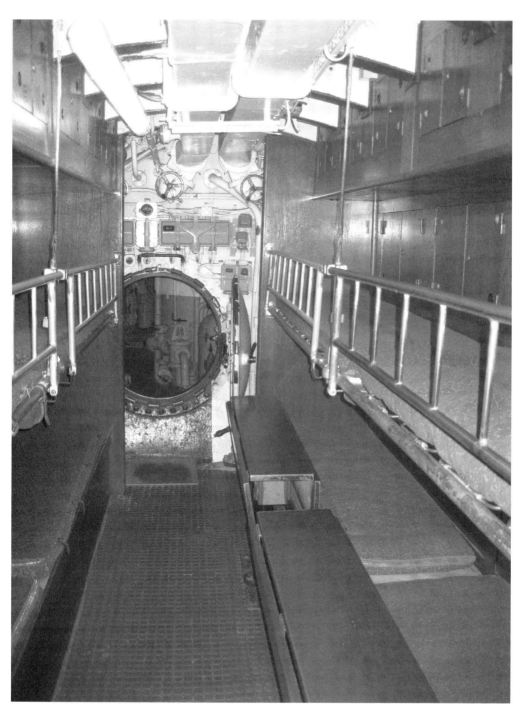

The petty officers' accommodation of *U-995* at Laboe near Kiel.

Above: The lavatory or heads in *U-534*.

Opposite above: The instructions on how to use the high-pressure heads in *U-534*.

Opposite below: *U-534*'s four-wheel coding machine with spare wheels in the box on the right.

Chapter 10

Operational Command

Before the war, Kapitän zur See und Kommodore Karl Dönitz set about creating a top-heavy U-boat administration so that he would end up end up with sufficient experienced men for whatever key positions might be required for any future event. This was streamlined once the Second World War began to make maximum use of available resources and, at around the same time, the U-boat flotillas became purely administrative units. Their wartime function was to look after boats and crews while in port. Their leaders had little or no operational role, except on a few occasions when there were intrusions into their immediate coastal waters. Once out of port, boats in the Atlantic came under the direct control of what was later called the U-boat Command and headed by Dönitz with Eberhard Godt as his Chief of Staff. The only exceptions were the fringe areas such as the Black Sea, the Mediterranean, the Arctic and later the Baltic, where flotilla commanders and flag officers for U-boats (*Führer der Unterseeboote* – F.d.U.) planned and conducted the battles.

It is important to emphasise that in 1935 Karl Dönitz became the commanding officer for operational U-boats only. At that time, school boats came under the jurisdiction of the Torpedo Inspectorate and Dönitz had nothing to do with U-boat construction. The U-boat Office within the Supreme Naval Command, with which Dönitz had no contact and which did not consult him on future planning, dealt with technical matters and submarine construction. This rather strange state of affairs was changed during the autumn of 1939, when the Supreme Commander-in-Chief of the Navy, Grand Admiral Erich Raeder, decreed that Dönitz should be consulted about future building processes.

Some years ago an English-language author introduced a significant mistake about the German command structure and others have since copied this to give the impression that flotilla commanders controlled operations at sea, which is totally wrong. Flotillas hardly ever operated as entire units like torpedo boats or minesweepers and once at sea each U-boat from the same flotilla could well operate independently in different areas. What was more, U-boat commanders from each flotilla may have known each other only in passing and have never trained together unless they had met earlier in some other group. The U-boat flotillas were very much on the same type of level as the land-based or 'stone' frigates of the Royal Navy that had no means of going to sea although their name was prefixed with the letters 'HMS'.

One of the big mistakes made by the U-boat Command after the start of the war was to reduce the number of men working in headquarters to the barest minimum to reduce the possibilities of infiltration by spies. There were a number of Admiralty staff officers, each with a specific task in the daily running of what was to become a complicated operational control department. It would seem that these men were so overworked that they did not have time to deal with all the papers that ended up on their desks and some had to be passed on without adequate scrutiny.

Orders to boats at sea were sent direct by radio and it was this link that provided the code breakers in the United Kingdom with one of their main insights into what was going on. This was especially detrimental for the Germans because boats were often sent to far-off areas without specific orders so that these would not be out-of-date by the time they arrived there. The latest instructions were then sent later by radio, often as lengthy communiqués.

Radio direction finders were nothing new. They had been around for long enough for even the least technically-minded officers to realise the source of any radio transmission could be determined by special units set up for that purpose. As far as the North Sea was concerned, Germany had three main radio direction finder stations. The most northerly was located at List on the Island of Sylt and there was another on the Island of Borkum close to the Dutch border with a third half way between the two at the old naval airship base at Nordholz near Cuxhaven. The last-mentioned provided a service to all shipping in the North Sea that might have got lost due to bad weather or whatever. Individual ships could call in by radio to ask for their position, which was calculated by simple triangulation from Sylt and Borkum. Each radio station, of course, could only determine the direction from which a signal was coming and was unable to work out a position without a bearing from another station. A knowledge of the distance and direction between the radio direction finders was obviously also required to calculate this with simple triangulation. This worked exceedingly well because these radio stations were connected by direct telephone line and could therefore issue an immediate bearing on any identifiable radio signal.

The weak link of this old-fashioned system was that each radio station had to identify at least part of the message to assure that they were all focussing in on the same source. This German system was functioning efficiently by the early 1930s and by that time it was common knowledge that Britain had also established a similar setup. What was more, Britain was known to have considerably longer base lines for their triangulation and could therefore obtain accurate results on positions much further out in the Atlantic.

To combat the possibility of ships at sea being detected by radio direction finders, the German Navy developed a short signal codebook with which it was possible to send commonly-used phrases by transmitting only a few letters of Morse code. These were so short that it was exceedingly difficult, if not impossible, for two radio direction finders to identify and to get a bearing on them. Towards the beginning of the war the German Radio Monitoring Service under Kapitän zur See Heinz Bonatz was reading much of the Royal Navy's codes and could thus determine that British positions of U-boats at sea were way off the mark. In fact the majority of errors were so great that it looked as if it was too difficult for Britain to obtain accurate positions for locations more than a few hundred miles from land. The fact that the German radio code was considered to be unbreakable and that Britain must have known the positions of all land-based radio stations led the German High Command into thinking that there was no danger of long messages from headquarters being of any use to an outsider. Once promoted to Konteradmiral, Dönitz approached the Naval High Command on several occasions with the suspicion that this was wrong and the Royal Navy was indeed reading the U-boat code. On each occasion 'experts' from the Supreme Naval Command found alternative weak links where the suspected leak could have come from and they assured him that it was impossible to break into the highly complicated Enigma code.

Despite these assurances, U-boat commanders remained suspicious and many refused to use their radio unless the enemy knew their position. Kapitänleutnant Otto Kretschmer of *U-99*, for example, got the nickname 'Silent Otto' not because he didn't speak but because he hardly ever used his radio. Routine messages piled up in the radio room and then when a victim advertised its position by sending a distress call Kretschmer would give permission for the waiting messages to be coded and transmitted. Radio receivers were usually left on, making it possible to pick up the majority of incoming messages so the boat was also in a position to receive the general hubbub of information for other boats.

Once boats were on their way back, the deep sea frequencies were changed to *Schaltung Küste* (Coastal Setting), so that the radio could pick up messages from the port or area they were making for. Once in port the commander would report to the appropriate flotilla leader and this was usually so informal that this person would be waiting for the U-boat on the dockside. While the commander attended a detailed debriefing, the engineer officer would hand a list of necessary repairs to the flotilla's engineer officer and any work approved by him would then be carried out. Although this sounds reasonably simple, there appear to have been some significant hurdles, with noteworthy disagreements about what needed to be done and enough logs contain comments that the repairs had been unsatisfactory. It is also worth emphasising recent comments on television that French workers were forced to repair U-boats. If this was true then it is difficult to explain how it came about that the French dockyards could turn incoming U-boats around much faster than their supposedly more enthusiastic German counterparts.

Several authors have missed a trick or two when dealing with U-boat attacks against shipping and have forgotten that for the first six months of the war U-boats were tied to the Prize Rules and although there were attempts to establish wolf packs, it was not until much later that these group attacks became a feature of the war at sea. Even the 'Happy Time' during the autumn of 1940 didn't see any significant patrol lines being established. Instead loose groups, formed by whatever U-boats happened to be in the area, converged on convoys that were being shadowed and in some cases produced the most astonishing results. These incredible successes came about as a result of the short-range, surface attack at night and not because wolf packs were being formed. The amazing point about these successes is that no one seems to have explained why they came to an abrupt end in December 1940. The weather has often been blamed, but a more detailed study of what exactly went on at sea does not yet appear to have been made and people have been content to digest the statistics of merchant ships sunk without taking into account the number of U-boats at sea.

The next significant step in the U-boats' demise occurred in March 1941, when four U-boats were sunk in rapid succession. Today we know that radar made a significant contribution to this state and it is quite likely that this was the reason U-boats achieved relatively poor results for the whole year. The number of ships sunk per U-boat at sea certainly dropped very dramatically. At this stage of the proceedings wolf packs started playing a significant role in the convoy war and it is important to remember that although the name usually appears in the singular, there were indeed three distinctly different types. In Germany they were called patrol lines, rather than wolf packs, and throughout 1941 it became obvious that Britain was doing splendidly in avoiding them. Convoys ran into the ends of these lines, so that only a few boats could get into position to intercept. Dönitz remarked in his diary that surprise and any advantages appeared to be always with the opposition and he suspected that an insight into his radio code was to blame. As has been said before, experts at the Supreme Naval Command rejected this hypothesis, saying it was impossible to break into the Enigma code. Yet the U-boat Command did apply sufficient pressure to change the system by adding a fourth wheel to the Enigma machines used in the Atlantic. Before this complicated system could be introduced on 1 February 1942, the U-boat Command also made a drastic change in the set-up of the patrol lines. Instead of forming almost motionless lines in the path of expected convoys, Dönitz created the so-called Fast Moving Patrol Line. Remaining totally motionless at sea is difficult because the boat loses its ability to steer, so the early patrol lines were arranged in such a way that the boats sailed in a long line abreast with just enough gaps between the boats to make it difficult for a ship to slip through without being seen. During the day they sailed towards the expected merchant ships and at night they changed direction to sail on the same heading, making it more difficult for ships to slip through in the darkness.

Guessing that the opposition was detecting the presence of the patrol lines, Dönitz changed tactics during early September 1941 to intercept Convoys SC42 and SC44, that were known to be on the way. Instead of lurking in their path, the U-boats were ordered to assemble to the south-west of Iceland and then move at fast cruising speed towards the merchant ships. This principle of the Fast Moving Patrol Line then remained in use until the entry of the United States into the war in December 1941 produced a change in the general approach.

The techniques of the wolf pack attack were changed once more in September 1943 when new weapons made it possible to attempt bolder methods of attack. By that time aircraft, especially those flown off improvised escort carriers, started making such significant inroads on the defence of convoys that many U-boats could not get close enough to launch an attack. The new weapons, introduced during the summer of 1943, were, first, a strengthening of the anti-aircraft guns and, secondly, the arrival of the acoustic torpedo that could cope with escorts approaching head-on at high speed. The Leuthen Pack was established on the western side of the Atlantic with orders for the boats to remain on the surface when their radar detectors indicated the presence of aircraft. Taking them on in gun duels, U-boats were supposed to continue towards their targets and only dive once they had aimed an acoustic torpedo at an approaching escort. This was necessary to prevent the torpedo homing in on the noise made by the U-boat. The distance between U-boat and target would have been several miles at that stage. Far enough away to be out of touch with what was happening on the surface and the detonation of the torpedo then suggested the escort had been sunk, while in reality they produced only an appalling 10 per cent success rate and this type of patrol line was also a significant failure.

Another point that has been sidestepped by historians is the role played by the code breakers at Bletchley Park. As soon as this secret came out, people were happy to jump on the bandwagon that this was the key to winning the war at sea. Yet people presenting this argument have conveniently forgotten that there had been an Atlantic blackout from 1 February 1942 until the end of year. Yet that period saw vast numbers of U-boats at sea and somehow they failed to find the convoys that were running around them. This state of affairs would suggest that the secret Submarine Tracking Room at the Admiralty in London under Rodger Winn was making a significant contribution to the successes at sea. At the same time the inroads made in the Western Approaches by Admiral Sir Percy Noble before Admiral Max Horten replaced him are usually hardly acknowledged.

Appendix 1

Wartime Statistics

Number of U-boats commissioned: 1,171

The figures for the following two tables have been calculated from Peter Sharpe's book *U-boat Fact File*, which was published in 1998. Although considerable new information has come to light since he compiled this book, the overall results should not have changed significantly.

Allied ships that were attacked and at least damaged:

38	U-boats attacked and at least damaged 20 or more ships
45	U-boats attacked and at least damaged 11–19 ships
72	U-boats attacked and at least damaged 6– 0 ships
307	U-boats attacked and at least damaged 1–5 ships
674	U-boats didn't get close enough to attack any ship

The number of operational voyages undertaken by U-boats:

Number of war voyages	Number of U-boats
0:	293
1:	262
2:	150
3:	101
4:	60
5:	54
6:	30
7:	32
8:	30

WARTIME STATISTICS

Number of war voyages	Number of U-boats
9:	27
10:	37
11:	16
12:	12
13–22:	29

It may also be significant to add that about 2 per cent of all U-boat commanders were responsible for 30 per cent of all Allied shipping sunk.

The following table shows ships and U-boats sunk by enemy action.

U-boats at sea = the average number of U-boats at sea each month. (Figures from Harald Busch, *U-Boats at War*, London: Hamilton, 1954 and New York: Putnam, 1954) and KTB des B.d.U.)

U-boats lost = Front line boats lost due to direct enemy action. Boats mined in home waters are not included. (Figures from Axel Niestlé, *German U-Boat Losses*, Barnsley: Frontline, 2014.)

Month	Ships sunk by U-boats	U-boats at sea	Ships sunk per U-boat at sea	U-boats Lost
Sep 1939	41	23	1.8	3
Oct	27	10	2.7	4
Nov	21	16	1.3	1
Dec	25	8	3.1	1
Jan 1940	40	11	3.6	2
Feb	45	15	3.0	5
Mar	23	13	1.8	3
Apr	7	24	0.3	4
May	13	8	1.6	1
Jun	58	18	3.2	1
Jul	38	11	3.5	2
Aug	56	13	4.3	2
Sep	59	13	4.5	1
Oct	63	12	5.3	1
Nov	33	11	3.0	2

Month	Ships sunk by U-boats	U-boats at sea	Ships sunk per U-boat at sea	U-boats Lost
Dec	37	10	3.7	0
Jan 1941	21	8	2.6	0
Feb	39	12	3.3	0
Mar	41	13	3.2	5
Apr	43	19	2.3	2
May	58	24	2.4	1
Jun	61	32	1.9	4
Jul	22	27	0.8	0
Aug	23	36	0.6	4
Sep	53	36	1.5	2
Oct	32	36	0.9	2
Nov	13	38	0.3	3
Dec	26	25	1.0	10
Jan 1942	62	42	1.5	3
Feb	85	50	1.7	2
Mar	95	48	2.0	6
Apr	74	49	1.5	3
May	125	61	2.0	4
Jun	144	59	2.4	3
Jul	96	70	1.4	11
Aug	108	86	1.3	9
Sep	98	100	1.0	9
Oct	94	105	0.9	16
Nov	119	95	1.3	12
Dec	60	97	0.6	5
Jan 1943	37	92	0.4	7
Feb	63	116	0.5	17
Mar	108	116	0.9	14
Apr	56	111	0.5	16
May	50	118	0.4	40
Jun	20	86	0.2	17

WARTIME STATISTICS

Month	Ships sunk by U-boats	U-boats at sea	Ships sunk per U-boat at sea	U-boats Lost
Jul	46	84	0.5	38
Aug	16	59	0.3	23
Sep	20	60	0.3	8
Oct	20	86	0.2	26
Nov	14	78	0.2	17
Dec	13	67	0.2	8
Jan 1944	13	66	0.2	14
Feb	18	68	0.3	17
Mar	23	68	0.3	23
Apr	9	57	0.2	19
May	4	43	0.1	21
Jun	11	47	0.2	26
Jul	12	34	0.4	20
Aug	18	50	0.4	33
Sep	7	68	0.1	20
Oct	1	45	0.0	11
Nov	7	41	0.2	7
Dec	9	51	0.2	13
Jan 1945	11	39	0.3	7
Feb	15	47	0.3	18
Mar	13	56	0.2	22
Apr	13	54	0.2	39
May	3	45	0.1	22

Appendix 2

The Attack U-boat Fleet

The following information:
Type (First launched – Last launched)
Description
In brackets, the number of boats launched, followed by identification numbers.

Boats were neither ordered, launched nor commissioned in logical numerical order for security reasons.

Type IA (1936)
Double-hulled, ocean-going submarine based on the Turkish *Gür*.
(2 launched)   U-25 & U-26

Type IIA (1935)
Small coastal submarine based on UB II (1915), UF (1918) and the Finnish *Vesikko*.
(6 launched)   U-1 – U-6

Type IIB (1935–6)
Modification of Type IIA.
The last two boats, built originally for export to China, were launched in 1940.
(20 launched)   U-7 – U-24
                            U-120 & U-121

Type IIC (1938–9)
Modification of Type IIB.
(8 launched)   U-56 – U-63

Type IID (1939–40)
Modification of Type IIC.
(16 launched)   U-137 – U-152

Type VIIA (1936)
Single-hulled, seagoing submarine based on UB III (1915–16) and the Finnish *Vetehinen*. Originally called just Type VII without the 'A'.
(10 launched)   U-27 – U-36

Type VIIB (1938–40)
Modification of Type VIIA.
(24 launched)   U-45 – U-55
                                 U-73 – U-76
                                 U-83 – U-87
                                 U-99 – U-102

Type VIIC (1940–4)
Modification of Type VIIB. An improved version, Type VIIC/41, was produced later during the war.
(Over 600 launched)

U-69 – U-72	U-825 – U-828
U-77 – U-82	U-901
U-88 – U-98	U-903 – U-908
U-132 – U-136	U-921 – U-930
U-201 – U-212	U-951 – U-1032
U-221 – U-232	U-1051 – U-1058
U-235 – U-329	U-1063 – U-1065
U-331 – U-458	U-1101 – U-1110
U-465 – U-486	U-1131 – U-1132
U-551 – U-683	U-1161 – U-1172
U-701 – U-722	U-1191 – U-1210
U-731 – U-779	U-1271 – U-1279
U-821 – U-822	U-1301 – U-1308

Type VIIC/41
Included with Type VIIC.

Type VIID (1941)
An enlarged version of Type VIIC with five mineshafts immediately aft of the conning tower.
(6 launched) U-213 – U-218

Type IXA (1938–9)
Double-hulled, ocean-going long-range multipurpose submarine developed from the First World War's *U-81*.
(8 launched) U-37 – U-44

Type IXB (1939–40)
Modification of Type IXA.
(14 launched) U-64 – U-65
  U-103 – U-111
  U-122 – U-124

Type IXC (1940–4)
Modification of Types IXA and IXB with a strengthened version. Type IXC/40 produced later during the war.
(143 launched) U-66 – U-68
  U-125 – U-131
  U-153 – U-176
  U-183 – U-194
  U-501 – U-550
  U-801 – U-806
  U-841 – U-846
  U-853 – U-858
  U-865 – U-870
  U-877 – U-881
  U-889 – U-891
  U-1221 – U-1235

Type IXC/40
Included with Type IXC.

Type IXD1 (1941–2)
Transport U-boat produced as an enlarged version of Type IXC with a very long range. Originally fitted with six high-speed E-boat engines which were not terribly successful.
(2 launched) U-180 & U-195

Type IXD-2 (1941–4)
Modified from Type IXC for very long range operations.
(30 launched)
U-177 – U-179
U-181 & U-182
U-196 – U-200
U-847 – U-852
U-859 – U-864
U-871 – U-876
U-883 – U-886

Appendix 3

Technical Data

	Type IIC–D	Type VIIC	Type IXC-IXC/40
Displacement ⇧:	291t	769t	1,120t
Displacement ⇩:	341t	871t	1,232t
Length:	43.9m	67.1m	76.76m
Beam:	4.08m	6.2m	6.76m
Depth:	3.82m	4.74m	4.7m
Diving Depth Max:	150m	200m	200m
Diving Time:	25 sec	27 sec*	35 sec
Speed ⇧ Max:	12kt	17.7kt	18.3kt
Speed ⇩ Max:	7kt	7.6kt	7.3kt
Range ⇧ Fast:	1,900nm/3,519km @ 12kt	3,250nm/5,926km @ 17kt	5,000nm/9,260km @ 18kt
Range ⇧ Cruise:	3,800nm/7,038km @ 8kt	8,500nm/15,742km @ 10kt	13,450nm/24,909km @ 10kt
Range ⇧ D/E:	4,200nm/7,778km @ 8kt	9,700nm/17,964km @ 10kt	16,800nm/31,113km @ 10kt
Range ⇩ Max speed:	43–56nm/80–104km @ 4kt	80nm/148km @ 4kt	63nm/116km @ 4kt
Range ⇩ Cruise:	100nm/185km @ 2kt	130nm/241km @ 2kt	128nm/ 37km @ 2kt
Torpedo Tubes Bow:	3	4	4
Torpedo Tubes Stern:	0	1**	2

TECHNICAL DATA

	Type IIC–D	Type VIIC	Type IXC-IXC/40
Torpedoes/Mines carried:	5 T or 18 TMB	14 T or 39 TMB	22 T or 66 TMB
Guns	1–2 x 20mm	1 x 88mm 1 x 20mm***	1 x 105mm 1 x 37mm 1 x 20mm
Crew, officers/men	3/22	4/40–56	4/44–56

⇑ = On surface
⇓ = Submerged
* = Achieved by the Royal Navy with the captured *U-570* renamed HMS *Graph*.
** = About half a dozen or so Type VIIC boats were built without a rear torpedo tube and some boats had them welded shut as a result of damage.
*** = The anti-aircraft armament was increased during the war.
D/E = Diesel/Electric drive
TMB = mines
kt = knots

U-518's run to American waters and back

The following table, although not easy to digest at first sight, is most interesting because it gives precise details of *U-518*'s voyage to the American side of the Atlantic. The boats'sengineer officer, Paul Weidlich, provided the information. In addition he also supplied details of the quantity of pure water produced by the boat's still. This worked on the simple principle of boiling seawater and then cooling the steam to produce what was often referred to as distilled water. When running for twenty-four hours the still produced 240 litres.

Days at sea
| Distance travelled on surface (nm)
| | Distance travelled submerged (nm)
| | | Time travelled on surface (hours-minutes)
| | | | Time travelled submerged (hours-minutes)
| | | | | Fuel used (cm$^{3)}$
| | | | | | Drinking water used (litres)

Days	↑ (nm)	↓ (nm)	↑ hr-min	↓ hr-min	cm^3	Litres
A	B	C	D	E	F	H
1	60	0	07-19	00-00	1.5	50
2	82	30	14-19	09-41	2.9	60
3	90	31	13-14	10-46	3.0	40
4	32	59	04-21	19-39	1.2	100
5	98	33	13-12	10-48	3.6	100
6	104	32	13-25	10-35	3.3	120
7	160	3	23-18	00-42	3.6	125
8	136	3	23-10	00-50	4.0	200
9	114	2.5	23-18	00-42	3.6	230
10	142	2	23-36	00-24	3.2	200
11	162	2.5	23-14	00-46	3.3	210
12	168	2	23-26	00-34	3.8	190
13	172	2.5	23-21	00-39	3.2	210
14	173	3	23-06	00-54	3.1	260
15	165	3.5	22-59	01-01	3.2	200
16	167	3	23-04	00-56	3.1	250
17	147	2	22-37	01-23	2.3	260
18	154	1.5	23-40	00-20	2.5	270
19	157	2	23-10	00-50	1.9	300
20	115	2	23-31	00-29	1.6	190
21	112	3	23-04	00-56	1.8	170
22	128	2	23-30	00-30	2.1	200
23	167	2	23-24	00-36	2.7	210
24	169	2.5	23-23	00-37	2.8	200
25	161	2.5	23-16	00-44	2.6	210

TECHNICAL DATA

Days	⬆ (nm)	⬇ (nm)	⬆ hr-min	⬇ hr-min	cm³	Litres
A	B	C	D	E	F	H
26	160	2	23-28	00-32	2.8	270
27	164	2	23-25	00-35	2.7	330
28	145	2	23-26	00-34	2.9	300
29	120	3	22-50	01-10	1.4	360
30	149	4	22-50	01-10	2.6	350
31	159	2	23-29	00-31	2.9	275
32	77	9	16-55	07-05	2.3	300
33	74	34	11-47	12-13	1.8	155
34	152	3	22-50	01-10	3.8	150
35	125	20	15-57	08-03	2.3	100
36	85	41	11-39	12-21	2.1	200
37	76	26	10-49	13-11	1.6	200
38	76	33	11-35	12-25	1.5	230
39	89	45	10-26	13-34	2.8	230
40	45	35	08-40	15-20	1.7	250
41	56	27	11-34	12-26	1.4	190
42	52	28	11-14	12-46	1.4	330
43	64	26	11-04	12-56	1.6	220
44	60	33	11-11	12-49	1.3	230
45	78	31	11-17	12-43	3.2	220
46	73	28	11-13	12-47	1.2	200
47	80	29	11-14	12-46	2.1	200
48	54	44	09-47	14-13	1.3	200
49	73	41	10-47	13-13	2.9	200
50	111	41	09-31	14-29	4.2	200
51	36	37	13-14	10-46	2.6	300
52	85	30	11-30	12-30	1.6	260
53	81	33	11-26	12-34	1.8	200
54	114	31	11-22	12-38	2.3	300
55	91	23	11-58	12-02	2.1	155
56	95	32	11-32	12-28	1.6	155

Days	↑ (nm)	↓ (nm)	↑ hr-min	↓ hr-min	cm³	Litres
A	B	C	D	E	F	H
57	80	39	11-26	12-34	1.7	135
58	68	32	11-23	12-37	1.7	200
59	70	25	10-59	13-01	2.2	315
60	80	38	11-23	12-37	1.7	200
61	67	45	11-29	12-31	1.7	240
62	74	38	12-11	11-49	2.5	190
63	57	29	11-18	12-42	1.5	110
64	63	38	10-07	13-53	2.0	190
65	100	39	11-26	12-34	2.2	260
66	87	26	11-14	12-46	2.4	150
67	88	31	10-32	13-28	2.4	120
68	106	33	10-14	13-46	4.1	135
69	81	30	09-52	14-08	2.6	160
70	73	32	09-59	14-01	1.7	200
71	75	27	11-05	12-55	1.6	140
72	76	34	11-16	12-44	1.5	150
73	58	44	08-38	15-22	1.2	160
74	73	39	09-30	14-30	2.7	180
75	69	30	10-26	13-34	1.4	270
76	73	30	11-11	12-49	1.6	230
77	71	30	11-13	12-47	1.4	220
78	64	28	10-39	12-21	1.5	200
79	70	32	12-31	11-29	1.7	210
80	82	46	09-08	14-52	1.9	180
81	186	2	23-34	00-26	2.8	150
82	164	0	24-00	00-00	2.4	190
83	158	2	23-28	00-32	2.2	160
84	158	2.5	23-27	00-33	2.4	190
85	164	2.5	23-21	00-39	2.4	190
86	166	2	23-23	00-37	2.5	200
87	166	2	23-35	00-25	2.4	195
88	153	2.5	23-21	00-39	2.5	165

TECHNICAL DATA

Days	⬆ (nm)	⬇ (nm)	⬆ hr-min	⬇ hr-min	cm³	Litres
A	B	C	D	E	F	H
89	140	2	23-29	00-31	2.6	130
90	137	1.5	23-34	00-26	2.5	195
91	136	2	23-29	00-31	2.5	195
92	128	2	23-21	00-39	2.6	180
93	130	2.5	23-21	00-39	2.8	120
94	125	6.5	23-22	00-38	2.6	200
95	12	48	12-25	11-35	0.8	180
96	122	21	23-12	00-48	2.6	230
97	162	2	23-32	00-28	2.7	370
98	173	9.5	21-06	02-54	3.7	200
99	186	2.5	23-24	00-36	3.9	160
100	115	33.5	13-23	10-37	2.3	190
101	98	34	09-59	14-01	2.5	140
102	95	36.5	09-33	14-27	1.6	130
103	96	36	09-35	14-25	2.5	120
104	85	39	09-44	15-16	2.2	135
105	84	36	09-45	15-15	2.2	240
106	87	35	09-08	15-52	2.2	300
107	89	0	09-46	00-00	2.0	300

Appendix 4

German Wartime Ranks

Seamen

Matrose	Ordinary Seaman
Matrosen~gefreiter	Able Seaman
Matrosen~ober~gefreiter	Leading Seaman
Matrosen~haupt~gefreiter	Leading Seaman with 4.5 years' service.
Matrosen~stabs~gefreiter and Matrosen~stabs~ober~gefreiter	Higher Leading Seaman ranks introduced during the war

Junior Non-Commissioned Officers without Swordknot (*Unteroffiziere ohne Portepee*), also known as Feldwebel

–maat	Petty Officer
Ober –maat	Chief Petty Officer

– The man's trade would have prefixed the word 'maat' to produce Funk~maat, Torpedo~maat, Maschinisten~maat etc,

An Ober – maat could not progress any higher up the promotion ladder without attending a long course and passing the stringent Warrant Officer School tests. There was one of these schools near Kiel and another for the North Sea Command in Wilhelmshaven.

Warrant Officers with Swordknot (*Unteroffiziere mit Portepee*)

Bootsmann	Boatswain
Ober~boots~mann	Chief Boatswain
Stabs~ober~boots~mann	Senior Chief Boatswain introduced during the war.

The man's trade would have been used instead of Boots~mann to produce Maschinist, Mechaniker, Funkmeister, etc.

This officer group was also known by the generic name of Feldwebel.

GERMAN WARTIME RANKS

Trainee Officers

Fähnrich zur See	Cadet/Midshipman
Ober~fähnrich zur See	Sub-Lieutenant

Commissioned Officers

Leutnant zur See	Lieutenant (Junior)
Oberleutnant zur See	Lieutenant (Senior)
Kapitänleutnant	Lieutenant Commander
Korvettenkapitän	Commander
Fregattenkapitän	Junior Captain
Kapitän zur See	Captain
Konteradmiral	Rear Admiral
Vizeadmiral	Vice Admiral
Admiral	Admiral
Grossadmiral	Admiral of the Fleet

Glossary

A: A code letter used by U-boats to denote a depth of 80m, the distance required for a surfaced submarine to level out after an emergency dive. Depths above it were usually referred to as A- (minus) and depths below it as A+ (plus). Thus 60m became A-20 and 110m A+30.

AA: Anti-aircraft.

aD: *ausser Dienst*. Withdrawn from service/retired.

Adam: A prototype midget submarine that went into production as Type *Biber*.

AGRU-Front: *Ausbildungs~gruppe-Front*. A technical division based in Hela near Danzig for operational training and testing of both machinery and men before going on to front-line duties. There were no hard and fast tests to be completed and the decision to pass was very much at the discretion of the officers conducting the tests. The staff was made up of experienced U-boat specialists.

Akku: Short for accumulator = battery.

Alberich **skin**: A code name for rubber sheets that covered U-boats to absorb Asdic impulses. At best it reduced sound impulses to 20 per cent of their strength and worked reasonably well, but it was too difficult to attach and often came off again, producing its own flapping noises. Used on only a few boats towards the end of the war.

AO: Artillery Officer.

Aphrodite: A foxer that reflected radar impulses.

Asdic: Now called Sonar; a device that could detect submerged submarines by sending out sound impulses and picking up the echo from the target.

GLOSSARY

ASV: Air to Surface Vessel. A cover name for an early type of radar that was used by the Royal Navy.

Athos: Code name for FuMB 25. A capstan-shaped radar detection aerial introduced on a few U-boats towards the end of the war. The upper ring with many small circular aerials picked up the 3cm and the lower ring with larger aerials picked up 9cm wavelengths.

Atlantic, the: Especially when comparing statistics it is important to remember that Germany tended to include the North Sea as part of the Atlantic, but for Britain it was part of the 'back garden' and was usually not included when dealing with the Atlantic.

B-Dienst: *Funk~beobachtungs~dienst*: Radio Monitoring Service.

Bachstelze: Wagtail. A gliding helicopter or autogyro without an engine that was raised into the air by the forward motion of the U-boat. Used mainly in the Indian Ocean towards the end of the war. It would seem that only one ship was sunk as a result of having been sighted by an observer in one of these craft. The Aeronauticum Museum at Nordholz near Cuxhaven has rebuilt a full-sized working model.

Back: Forecastle.

Backbord: Port side of a ship.

Bali: An aerial for radar detectors of Type *Borkum* and *Samos*.

Basis Nord: A German base in Russia that was supposed to have been used by U-boats from November 1939 until shortly after the invasion of Norway. It was situated a short distance west of Polijarny near Murmansk.

BBC: Brown Boveri & Co. A Swiss firm that produced electrical switching gear for the German Navy. The initials are often seen on photographs showing the steering and hydroplane controls.

Befehlshaber: Commanding Officer or Commander-in-Chief

Befehlshaber der Unterseeboote: B.d.U., Commander-in-Chief for U-boats

Begleit~schiff: Escort ship.

Bei~boot: Ship's boat or longboat. Could also mean tender.

BETASOM: The Italian U-boat Command for the Atlantic based in Bordeaux (France) and founded in September 1940. The name was derived from '*Beta*' meaning base and '*Sommergibili*', Italian for submarine. Dönitz did not want to provide the Italians with an excuse to command German U-boats in the Mediterranean and therefore created this autonomous Italian command for Italian U-boats operating in the Atlantic.

Bib`er: 'Beaver'. A midget submarine developed from the prototype *Adam*.

'Biscay Cross': A self-made, improvised aerial for the *Metox* radar detector.

Bletchley Park: The home of the British code breakers. Now a museum near Milton Keynes.

Bold: An Asdic foxer that was ejected through a small tube in the stern of U-boats to produce a mass of bubbles in the water. This reflected sound impulses to confuse Asdic operators. Introduced during 1942 as a result of many submerged U-boats being driven away when attacking convoys.

Boots~mann: Boatswain – Often a warrant officer with *Portepee* (Swordknot).

Boots~manns~maat: Boatswain's assistant – A petty officer without *Portepee* (Swordknot).

Borkum: A code name for a radar detector of Type FuMB 10 or the most westerly of the German Frisian Islands on the Dutch border near Emden.

BRT: *Brutto Register Tonnen*: GRT = Gross Register Tonnage.

Bug: Bows.

Crew: The class or year when officers joined the navy.

'Curly': The British identification for German torpedoes that looped through convoys. See FAT and LUT

Cypern: 'Cyprus'. Code name for W-ANZ 2 – a radar detector. See Wanze.

D-Maschine: Diesel engine.

Deadlight, Operation: The scuttling/sinking of German U-boats after the war by the Royal Navy.

Delphin: Experimental midget U-boat.

Destroyer: The Germans tended to use this term for describing most small fast warships used for hunting U-boats.

GLOSSARY

DeTe Gerät: *Dezimeter~telefonie~gerät*, which was also called *Dreh~turm~gerät* by many who didn't know the correct name. An early type of radar that was developed during the early 1930s.

Deutsche Werke: A shipyard in Kiel where the first Second World War U-boats were assembled in 1935, which should not be confused with Deutsche Werft in Hamburg-Finkenwerder.

Dräger: A firm that made emergency breathing devices for coal miners and later developed the German submarine escape apparatus (Dräger Lung).

E-Maschine: Electric motors.

Eel: German slang for torpedo.

Einbaum: 'Dugout', an early nickname for Type II U-boats. They were also called 'North Sea Ducks'.

Elefant: A midget submarine also known as *Seeteufel* of which only a few experimental models were built. It had tank tracks so that it could launch itself from firm beaches.

Elektro-U-boot: U-boats of Type XXI and XXIII that were capable of fast underwater speeds by accommodating a large number of batteries.

EMA, EMB, EMC etc.: *Einheits~mine Typ* A, B and C. Standard mine types that were developed during the First World War.

EMS: A mine that was developed during the Second World War with what looked like an extended periscope sticking out of the water to hopefully attract submarine chasers to ram it. Not successful because it was easy to recognise due to there being no wash.

Engelmannboot = **VS5**: An experimental submarine for testing new high-speed engines.

Enigma: A generic name for the German code machine that was used by all the armed forces, with a special version for U-boats. Also known as *Schlüssel~maschine M* meaning Coding Machine M (M = Marine (Navy)).

Ersatz: Substitute or replacement, often used for cheaper wartime products of inferior quality.

Escort Carrier: An improvised aircraft carrier. Many were built by removing the superstructure from merchant ships and adding a flight deck. These were most effective against U-boats from the late autumn of 1941 onwards and played a significant role in the Battle of the Atlantic.

Escort Group: Allied warships that escorted convoys and operated as a group under command of an escort commander.

Falke: A forerunner of the acoustic *Zaunkönig* torpedo.

FAT: *Feder~apperat~torpedo*. An anti-convoy torpedo called 'Curly' in Britain. Also referred to in Germany by the wrong name of *Flächen~absuchenden~torpedo* (surface-searching torpedo).

F.d.U.: *Führer der Unterseeboote*. Flag Officer for U-boats.

Feindfahrt: Operational voyage rather than a training exercise.

Flak: *Flug* or *Flieger~abwehr~kanone*; Anti-aircraft gun.

Flakboot: Anti-aircraft boat; could have been a submarine or surface vessel.

Fliege: A radar detector.

Flieger~führer Atlantik: Commander for Aircraft in the Atlantic, not a naval position but held by a Luftwaffe officer.

Flug~zeug~falle: Aircraft trap.

FMB, FMC: *Flussmine Typ* B and C: River Mine. Developed during the 1930s.

Freikorps Dönitz: Free Corps Dönitz – a nickname for the U-boat Arm.

Freya Gerät: An early radar set that was especially good at detecting aircraft and used as such mainly by the Luftwaffe. It worked on a 2.4 metre wavelength.

Führer: Leader/Commander/Flag Officer, usually with the rank of captain.

FuMB: *Funk~mess~beobachtung*: detection of radar signals.

FuME: *Funk~mess~erkennung*: radar recognition.

FuMG: *Funk~mess~gerät*: radio rangefinder/radar apparatus.

FuMO: *Funk~mess~ortung*: radar.

Funk: radio/radio telegraphy.

Funk~beobachtungs~dienst: B-Dienst: Radio Monitoring Service.

Funk~aufkärung: Radio Monitoring or B-Dienst.

Funker: Radio operator.

Funk~mess: Radar.

G7a, G7e, G7v: German torpedoes.

Geheim~rat: Privy councillor, not secret adviser.

Geleit: Convoy.

Germania~werft: Germania Works. Founded in 1876 in Kiel and taken over by the Krupp steel firm from Essen in 1883. Built a number of warships before the First World War. Around the beginning of the twentieth century it had the only large slipways in Germany that were covered by a huge glass hangar for the purpose of building torpedo boats, but the hangar was used mainly for the construction of U-boats during both world wars. Howaldtswerke now occupies the site and a new ferry terminal has been built over another part of the old shipyard.

Glückauf: A development bureau founded in 1943 for designing new submarine types.

Goliath: Name of a large radio transmitter near Magdeburg, which could reach U-boats submerged off America's east coast. Russian forces dismantled much of it after the war.

GRT: Gross Register Tonnage: BRT in German.

Grund~ausbildung: Initial military training.

Gruppen~horch~gerät: GHG. A passive sound detector used by the German Navy in U-boats and surface ships and capable of hearing engine noises of ships that were too far away for U-boat lookouts to see.

Gruppen~taktik: Group tactics, patrol lines, wolf pack tactics.

H/F D/F: High Frequency Direction Finder also called Huff Duff. (HF/DF is a post-war introduction, probably used by authors who were not aware that the original was different.

Hafen: (-haven). Port/harbour. The Kaiser decreed that inland ports and those on the Baltic whose name includes this noun should be written with an 'f' and harbours on the North Sea should be written with a 'v'. Whence Wilhelmshaven and Gotenhafen.

Heads: Lavatory – usually in the plural even when there is only one.

Hecht: The prototype of the two-man *Seehund* midget submarine.

Hedgehog: An ahead-throwing mortar used by surface ships against submerged U-boats. The bombs exploded on impact. Similar to the American Mousetrap but with the propelling charge inside the bottom of the firing tube. The backfire produced was so considerable that it could only be used on ships with strong decks. Twenty-four separate charges could be fired according to a predetermined pattern. Exploding on impact had the great advantage over depth charges inasmuch that it was not necessary to wait until the noise and water disturbance subsided before regaining Asdic contact and the attack could continue unabated until an explosion, powerful enough to crack the pressure hull, indicated a hit. See also Mousetrap.

Heizer: Stoker. A seaman from the technical division with the lowest rank. An old-fashioned term inherited from the Imperial Navy.

Hertha: A code name for the new Type XXI large electro-U-boats.

Hohentwiel: FuMB 65: A rotating bedstead-like aerial for detecting radar impulses, often with radar aerials on the reverse side.

Horch~torpedo: Acoustic torpedo.

Huff Duff: See H/F D/F = High Frequency (Radio) Direction Finder.

Hunter Killer Group: Groups of small warships introduced by the United States to hunt U-boats to destruction, rather than concentrating on guarding convoys.

Hydrophone: Underwater microphone.

Hydroplane: Blades on the outside of a submarine for controlling depth, similar to elevators on an aircraft.

iD: *in Dienst~stellung*. Commissioning, commissioned.

Ing: *Ingenieur*. Engineer.

Ingenieurs~büro Glückauf: See Glückauf.

Ingenieurs~büro voor Scheepsbouw: IvS. A German construction bureau in Holland set up at a time when Germany was not allowed to build or own submarines.

Ingolin: Hydrogen peroxide – used as fuel and named after the son of Dr Hellmuth Walther.

K-Verband = *Klein~kampf~verband*: Midget Weapons Unit.

Kaleu/Kaleunt: An accepted colloquialism of Kapitän~leutnant. Since the English word 'sir' does not feature in German, people would have said 'Herr -' and then the person's rank. It has been suggested in books that *Kaleu* was an official position within a U-boat, which is not correct. *Kaleu* or *Kaleunt* were not used in written communications; neither was there a position in U-boats called 'the *Kaleu*'.

GLOSSARY

Kali~patrone: Breathing apparatus containing potash that absorbed carbon dioxide. The device was worn around the chest with a pipe connection to the mouth. Later during the war this was replaced by fitting such apparatus to the walls rather than each man having to wear the device.

Kapitän (zur See): The master of a merchant ship held the position of Kapitän while a captain of a large warship held the rank of Kapitän zur See.

Klein~kampf~mittel: Midget weapons.

Klein~kampf~verband: Midget Weapons Unit.

Kommandant: The commanding officer of a sea-going unit.

Kommandeur: The commanding officer of a land-based unit.

Kommando: Command

Koralle: Code name for a bunker in Bernau near Berlin used by the Naval and U-boat Command towards the end of the war before moving to Plön and then to the Naval Officers' School in Mürwik.

Korfu: A radar detector working on the 9cm waveband that was introduced during the early autumn of 1943.

Kriegs~marine: The name of the German Navy from 1935 until the end of the war. The navy called itself Marine rather than Kriegsmarine.

Kriegs~metal: A cheap wartime metal of inferior quality.

KTB: *Kriegs~tage~buch*, War diary. In U-boats it had to be signed by the commanding officer every four hours and was regarded as an official document.

Kurz~signal: Short (radio) signal.

Laboe: A small town near Kiel where the Naval Memorial is located.

Leigh Light: A searchlight fitted to aircraft hunting U-boats, capable of illuminating ships at a distance of several miles and used in close combat.

Leutnant zur See: A naval Leutnant had the suffix 'zur See' while other services used the rank without any additions.

LI: *Leitender Ingenieur*: Engineer officer.

'Lord': A nickname for the men with the lowest ranks.

Luft~torpedo: Aerial torpedo. These were slightly smaller than the standard naval version.

LUT: *Lagen~unabhängigen~torpedo*. A further development of FAT and called 'Curly' by the Royal Navy.

Maat: Petty Officer (always without *Portepee* – Swordknot).

Marder: Midget submarine.

Marine: The German Navy, although officially known as Kriegsmarine and earlier as Reichsmarine and before that as Kaiserlichemarine, usually referred to itself as just Marine.

Maschinist: Mechanic/engineer.

Matrose: Ordinary Seaman with lowest rank or sailor.

Meister: Master of a trade; was used for some warrant officer ranks.

Metox: A long-wave radar detector that used the Biscay Cross before U-boats were fitted with a new circular type of aerial. Named after the French firm that built it and known in Germany also as FuMB 1.

Milch~kuh: Milk cow. Supply U-boat also known as *Seekuh*.

Molch: Midget submarine.

Möltenort: A small town near Kiel where the U-boat Memorial is situated.

Mousetrap: An ahead-throwing mortar for anti-submarine bombs that exploded on impact. Similar to a Hedgehog, except that the propelling charge was in the projectile and not in the bottom of the firing tube. The Americans developed this for use on ships with weak decks, which could be damaged by the powerful backfire of a Hedgehog.

Mücke: A radar detector.

Naxos: A radar detector that was introduced during the summer of 1943 and officially known as FuMB 7.

Neger: Midget submarine.

Niebelung: An underwater detection device that was introduced towards the end of the war and also called *S-Anlage* = S-Installation.

Nordsee~enten: 'North Sea Ducks' an early nickname for Type II U-boats.

Not~ausblase~luft: Emergency air inlet for blowing diving tanks.

ObdM: *Ober~befehls~haber der Marine*; Supreme Commander-in-Chief of the Navy.

Ober~boots~mann: Chief Boatswain – A warrant officer with *Portepee* (Swordknot).

GLOSSARY

Ober~steuer~mann: Navigator not helmsman. In a U-boat he doubled up as Third Watch Officer and was usually a warrant officer with *Portepee* (Swordknot). This was the lowest rank of this trade in U-boats, which did not employ an ordinary *Steuer~mann* – plural = *Steuer~männer*.

Ober~maat: Chief Petty Officer – always without *Portepee* (Swordknot).

OKM: *Ober~kommando der Marine*, Supreme Naval Command with its headquarters in Berlin until it was bombed out during November 1943, then moved to a nearby bunker.

OKW: *Ober~kommando der Wehrmacht*, Supreme Headquarters of the Armed Forces.

Opium: Opium was carried by U-boats and other ships where men had to remain on duty for 24 hours or more, sometimes for two days or more. Opium prevented them from having to sit on the heads for any length of time by blocking the digestive system. Pills that prevented them from going to sleep were carried as well.

Panzer~schrank: An armoured cupboard on the top of the conning tower to serve as shelter against gunfire from aircraft. These were not terribly successful and not many were fitted.

Patrol Line: wolf pack.

Pauken~schlag, **Operation**: Code name for the first U-boat attack against the United States. The word cannot be translated into English and has a more precise meaning than a roll on the kettledrums, but that would be the best translation.

Peil~gerät: Direction Finder.

Portepee: **Swordknot** – an award for warrant and commissioned officers that was tied onto the handle of daggers and swords. Gold for commissioned officers and silver for warrant officers.

Pressure hull: The strong thick steel hull that prevented a submarine from being crushed by water pressure. Fairings and tanks on the outside of this pressure hull were open to the sea so that water could penetrate into those spaces to allow the pressure inside to be the same as the water on the outside.

Radar: From Radio Detection and Ranging; called *Funk~mess* in German.

Radio Direction Finder: A radio receiver with a directional aerial that could determine the bearing from which radio signals were coming from. Used by the Germans especially during periods of bad weather to find the direction in which a convoy-shadowing U-boat was located.

Raum~not~luft: An external air inlet for ventilating the interior of a submarine in emergencies.

Regen~bogen: A code word used towards the end of the war meaning that ships of the German Navy should be scuttled to prevent them from falling into enemy hands.

Reichs~marine: The name of the German Navy from shortly after the First World War until 1935.

Reichs~mark: German currency until the shortly after the end of the Second World War.

Rotterdam Apparatus: A British short-wave radar set found by the Germans in an aircraft shot down near Rotterdam on 12 February 1943.

Rudel~taktik: Group tactics or wolf packs.

Ruder~gänger: Helmsman.

S-Anlage: An active underwater detection device with the code name Nibelung that was introduced towards the end of the war. It was fitted to some Type XXI boats.

S-Boot: *Schnell~boot* Motor Torpedo Boat; known as E-boat (Enemy Boat) in English.

Samoa: An aerial and radio/radar detector.

Samos: Radar detector.

Schacht~mine: Shaft mine carried in wet tubes by some U-boats such as the Type XB and Type VIID minelayers. See SMA.

Schlüssel M: Key M – the Enigma radio code used by the navy.

Schnorchel: German for Schnorkel. Snort in America. Snorkel has also crept in, but is a misspelling that appeared after the war.

See~kriegs~leitung: SKL, Naval War Staff.

See~teufel: Experimental midget submarines. Only a few were built. Also known as *Elefant*.

See~hund: Midget submarine with a crew of two.

See~kuh: Supply U-boat more often known as *Milch~kuh*.

Short signal: The Germans had a short radio signal codebook with which it was possible to condense commonly-used words and phrases

GLOSSARY

into a few letters of Morse code. These were thought to have been too short for conventional radio direction finders to get bearings on and were thus considered to be safe when used away from coastal waters. However, High Frequency Direction Finders (H/F D/F = Huff Duff) was capable of getting a bearing on these and this played a highly significant role during the war.

SMA, SMB: *Schacht~mine*: Shaft Mine Type A or B. Mines used by the large Type XB and VIID minelayers. These were stored in tubes that flooded when the boat dived and therefore the crew did not have access to them for making adjustments at sea.

Smut/Smutje: Cook

Snorkel: Misspelling for Schnorkel.

Sonar: An echo ranging device that was called Asdic during the Second World War. The apparatus sent out an audible ping and could determine the position of a submerged object by picking up the echo.

Sonar buoy: Introduced towards the end of the Second World. Several sonar buoys with automatic radios were dropped, often from aircraft to help locate underwater objects.

Spargel: 'Asparagus'. German slang for periscope.

Spatz: 'Sparrow'. Nickname for rescue buoys, each with a lamp and often with telephone as well, that were fitted to U-boats before the war and to some training boats during the war. The buoy could be blown out of its fitting by depth charges and was therefore removed from operational boats at the outbreak of hostilities.

Squid: An ahead-throwing mortar for hunting submerged submarines. The launcher was located at the stern of the ship where large projectiles were thrown over the bridge to hit the water some distance ahead. Each projectile weighing about 390lb contained 207lb of explosives. These could be fired extremely accurately with a new type of Asdic that automatically set the correct depth just a few seconds before firing. Introduced by the Allies towards the end of the war, this weapon remained on the highly secret list until some time after the end of the war and captains were warned not to use the Squid under any circumstances if there were war correspondents on board who might witness this in action.

Stamm: Personnel when referring to men who are not commissioned officers.

Stapel~lauf: Launch.

Steuer~bord: Starboard – The right-hand side of a ship.

Steuer~mann: Could mean helmsman on a large ship or in the merchant navy. Not used in U-boats as the majority had a warrant officer of higher rank with the title of *Ober~steuer~mann*, who was the third watch officer or navigator.

Sumatra: An aerial of a radar detector.

T5: The *Zaunkönig* acoustic torpedo.

Tauch~retter: Submarine escape apparatus.

TEK: *Torpedo~erprobungs~kommando*, Torpedo Trials Command.

Thetis: A radar foxer that consisted of a three-dimensional cross that floated on the surface of the water to confuse enemy radar.

TMA, TMB, TMC: Torpedo Mine Type A, B or C.

TO: Torpedo Officer.

Trim dive: Shortly after leaving port and every time heavy weights were moved it was necessary to dive so that the engineer officer could balance the submarine to sit correctly in the water. This was done by moving water around a complicated system of tanks.

Tunis: Code name for the FuMB 26 radar detector that was used towards the end of the war.

Turm: Tower – on a submarine the conning tower.

TVA: *Torpedo~versuchs~anstalt*, Torpedo Experiments/Trials Institute. Operational as part of the Torpedo Inspectorate for building, testing and evaluating new designs.

U-boot: From *Unter~see~boot* meaning submarine. In Britain the term tends to be used to describe submarines belonging to the Axis Powers while Allied craft were always referred to as submarines.

U-boot~abwehr~schule: Submarine Defence or Anti-Submarine School set up in Kiel at a time when Germany was not allowed to own or build submarines. This was a cover for training future submarine personnel.

U~boot~amt: U-boat Office – A department within the Supreme Naval Command responsible for designing and supervising the building of U-boats. The many authors who claim that Karl Dönitz was responsible for building U-boats before the war are way off beam. He had nothing to do with planning or building until after the start of the war.

GLOSSARY

U-boot~ausbildung: U-boat training.

U-boot~bunker: U-boat bunker.

U-boot~falle: U-boat trap = Q-ship.

U-boot~jäger: Submarine hunter.

U-boot~kreuzer: U-boat cruiser – Large U-boats that were never built. Sometimes also used to describe very-long-range Type IXD-2 boats.

U-boots~führung: U-boat leadership = U-boat Command.

UB: The German identification of HMS *Seal* that was captured around the beginning of the war. Also a series of attack submarines from the First World War.

UC: Used as identification for Norwegian submarine that were commissioned into the German Navy during the Second World War and for mine-laying submarines of the First World War.

UD: Identification for Dutch submarines that were commissioned into the German Navy during the Second World War.

UF: French submarines that were commissioned into the German Navy during the Second World War.

UIT: Italian submarines with German crews that served in the German Navy during the Second World War.

ULD: *U-boot~lehr~division*. Not part of the submarine training process but an accommodation unit for fully-trained men waiting for a posting to a specific U-boat.

UMA, UMB, UMC: *U-boot~abwehr~mine*: Submarine Defence Mines.

Ursel Project: A device developed towards the end of the Second World War but not made operational. It was designed to shoot rockets at small warships that were hunting U-boats.

UT Anlage: *Unter~wasser~telefonie*. Underwater communication equipment.

UZO: *U-boot~ziel~objekt*. U-boat torpedo sight on the top of the conning tower with special water and pressure resisting binoculars that were clipped on top when required.

Valentin: Name of a large bunker at Farge on the River Weser that was never completed but intended to cover an assembly line for the new Type XXI U-boats.

Verband: Unit.

Versuchs~kommando **456**: An experimental command for midget weapons founded towards the end of the war by Admiral Hellmuth Heye.

Verwaltung: Administration.

VHF: Very High Frequency (radio).

Vorläufig: Provisional.

Vorschiff: Bows/Forecastle.

VS5: See Engelmannboot.

Wabos: *Wasser~bomben*, depth charges.

Walter~boot: One of the new high-speed boats using hydrogen peroxide as fuel that were developed by Hellmuth Walter.

Wanze = W-Anz: *Wellen~anzeiger*, Frequency Indicator/Receiver. A radar detector that automatically searched through a variety of wavelengths. Developed as a successor to the earlier *Metox* radar detector.

Welle: Wave on the surface of the water or propeller shaft.

Werft: Shipyard, but would also apply to aircraft building/repair establishments.

Werkstatt~schiff: Depot ship/workshop boat/repair ship.

Wik: A sandy bay and the name of the part of Kiel where the main naval base is located.

Wintergarden: Conservatory – Slang for the anti-aircraft gun platforms on U-boats.

Wolf pack: Patrol line or group of U-boats working together to hunt convoys.

Wolfs~rudel: Wolf pack/Patrol line.

Woll~hand~krabbe: A woolly crab that was brought to Europe from the Far East that is capable of tolerating salt and fresh water and considered to have been a pest. Used as slang for Swastika.

Zaun~könig: The T5 acoustic anti-destroyer torpedo.

Zentrale: Central Control Room.

Index

accidental sinkings, 31
acoustic torpedo failures, 229
air compressors, 124
aircraft hitting back, 86
aircraft traps, 90
alarm bells in diesel room, 121
Alberich skin, 103
anchor motor, 62
Anglo-German Naval
   Agreement, 44
anti-aircraft armament,
   improved, 41
Aschmoneit, Christoph, 83, 85
Asdic, 15, 39

ballast pump, 169
Bartenbach, Karl, 22
'Biscay Cross', 80
Bletchley Park, 139
Bonatz, Heinz, 226
Brink, Heinrich, 122
Britton, Professor Gus, 114

capstan, 58, 62
circle with cross, 85
codes, British reading U-boat, 40
Compton-Hall, Richard, 114

Coward of the Day, 185
'Curly' torpedo, 109

Dahlmann, *Obersteuermann*, 179
Das Boot, 121
DeTe Apparatus, 101
diesel engines, new types, 22
dinghy for U-boats, 60
dog watches, 191
Dutch Navy, 103

Enders, Gerd, 114
Enigma machines, 228
escort carriers, 228
escort commanders, 40

Fast Moving Patrol Line, 228
Feldwebel, 181
Finland, 15
   financial package for, 25
flagpoles, 88
flexible connections, 50

Godt, Eberhard, 203
Gröner, Erich, 57
Group Listening Device,
   59, 62

Gurkha Board of Honours, 15
gyrocompass, 21

Haupt, *Obersteuermann*, 180
heads, 39
H/F D/F, 40
Hohentwiel aerial, 81
'Huff Duff' *see* H/F D/F
hydrophones *see* sound detector

Iku-Turso, 20
Imperial War Museum, 12
Italian submarine plans, 29

jumping wires, 59

Kaleu, 189
Kaleunt, 189
Kleyer, *Obersteuermann*, 179
Köhl, Fritz, 57
Königsberg, cruiser, 97
Korth, Claus, 52
Kretschmer, Otto, 99

Lagoda, Lake 22
Launt, Lt.z.S., 193
Lemp, Julius, 86
Lindberg, Lennart, 57
long-range U-boats, 53
lookouts, 82

Maritime Museum Zeebrugge, 110
Marks, Friedrich-Karl, 186
Medway, River, 7
Metox radar detector, 80
mooring bollards, 64
Müller, Matrosengefreiter, 174
Munzer, Gustav, 83
muscle power, 29, 34
Mützelburg, Rolf, 190

Naval Memorial, 83
new type of submarine, 41
Niestlé, Axel, 57

outboard engines, 60

patrol lines, 228
periscopes, 25
Prize Rules, 227
propellers on *U534*, 66

radar, 40
radio direction finder, 45, 225
Radio Monitoring
  Service, 226
Raeder, Erich, 25
railings on U-boats, 58
rain gear, 80
rescue buoys, 58

Saltzwedel, 89
Schepke, Joachim, 99
Schnee, Adalbert, 182
Schnorkel, 42
sextants, 180
short signal code book, 226
short-range attack, 43
sinkings, accidental, 31
Sobe, Ernst, 87
sound detector, 58, 59, 62
spare parts, 124
Spatz (Sparrow), 67
square with cross, 85
Steinhoff, Friedrich, 115
sunk by aircraft, 59
surface night attack, 43

Thwaites, Richard, 74
Topp, Erich, 43, 44, 52
torpedo detonator, 155

INDEX

torpedo loading cradle, 22
tow ropes, 58
Turkish submarine plans, 29
Type I, 44
Type XXI, 42
Type XXIII, 42

U-9, 179
U-20, 68
U-25, 203
U-30, 86, 90
U-31, 59
U-32, 45, 89
U-34, 87
U-42, 58
U-47, 85
U-53, 58, 84
U-57, 43, 44
U-58, 103
U-67, 103
U-73, 47
U-81, 53
U-93, 52
U-98, 122
U-99, 99
U-100, 99
U-107, 57
U-108, 179
U-172, 48, 101
U-201, 182
U-203, 180
U-203, 190
U-236, 103

U-357, 51
U-376, 186
U-505, 169
U-511, 115
U-515, 64
U-518, 125
U-534, 66, 79, 102
   U-534 Museum, 216
U-552, 52
U-570, 39, 68
U-673, 90
U-755, 71
U-870, 78
U-889, 91, 102, 104, 105, 125, 148, 195
UB-10, 13
UB-40, 4
UB-49, 5
UB-57, 6
UB-65, 17
UB-122, 3, 7
UB-126, 7
U-boat radio code, 40

Vesihiisi, 20
Vetehinen, 20, 47

washing in U-boats, 39
watch changes on U-boats, 191
Weidlich, Paul, 125
Wichers, J.J., Commander, 103
wind-free eddy, 85

XXIII loading cradle, 22